SELECTIONS FROM
NEHRU

SELECTIONS FROM
NEHRU

Edited by

GANESWAR MISHRA
SARAT CHANDRA SATAPATHY

Orient Longman

ORIENT LONGMAN LIMITED

Registered Office :
3-6-272 Himayatnagar, Hyderabad 500 029, (A.P.) INDIA

Other Offices :
Bangalore / Bhopal / Bhubaneshwar / Chandigarh /
Chennai / Ernakulam / Guwahati / Hyderabad / Jaipur /
Kolkata / Lucknow / Mumbai / New Delhi / Patna

Third Impression 1990
Reprinted 1994
Reprinted (Twice) 1995
Reprinted 1996, 1997, 1998, 1999, 2000, 2001

ISBN 81 250 0319 3

Printed in India by
Jai Hind Press
Patna 800 020

Published by
Orient Longman Ltd.
Govind Mitra Road ·
Patna 800 004

CONTENTS

PREFACE

JAWAHARLAL NEHRU, the great freedom fighter and the first Prime Minister of free India for seventeen years, is one of the noblest men of Indian history. It is almost impossible to think of modern India without Nehru.

An educated Indian is generally aware of Nehru's life and achievements. Born in Allahabad in 1889, the only son of Motilal Nehru, the veteran freedom fighter and prosperous lawyer, and Swarup Rani, Jawaharlal had his education at Harrow and Cambridge. When he was twenty he took his second class tripos in Science at Cambridge and, for some time, thought of preparing for the Indian Civil Service. But he rejected that idea and got through the Bar examinations, 'with neither glory nor ignominy'. He returned to India, after spending seven years in England and joined the Allahabad High Court.

Those were the days of great turmoil arising from the freedom struggle. Gandhi had already returned from South Africa after launching successfully his civil disobedience movement against the oppressive and racist South African government. The Congress was active and the Indian masses had recognized in Gandhi a form of dynamic leadership that they had never known before. Nehru, a lover of freedom and a keen student of history and public affairs, was inspired by Gandhi and joined the Congress. Soon he found himself in the midst of active public life and emerged as the undisputed leader of tthe Indian people, second perhaps only to Gandhi.

During the freedom struggle Nehru spent several years in prison and suffered from various personal setbacks. He lost his wife, Kamala, in 1936. But his total commitment to the cause of freedom and upliftment of the countrymen sustained him. Finally, India won her independence and Nehru became the first Prime Minister and the responsibility of leading the new nation fell on his shoulders.

As Prime Minister, Nehru was the chief architect of India's

economic and foreign policies. He zealously championed the cause of socialism and non-alignment. He had great faith in democracy and science and his government strove to establish communal harmony and economic justice. Even after his death in 1964, successive Indian governments have hardly deviated from the policies framed by Nehru.

Nehru was a man of action and in the midst of his hectic public life and heavy official engagements could hardly find time to devote himself to writing. Yet he has produced works like *Letters from a Father to his Daughter* (1930), *Glimpses of World History* (1934), *An Autobiography* (1936), and *The Discovery of India* (1946), which are classics of their kind. These books were written in prison when Nehru had long periods of isolation and he utilized the time mostly in reading and writing.

An Autobiography, written during 1934-35, is a narration of the events of his public and private life. In the preface this is how he explains the purpose of writing such a book:

> ...The primary object in writing these pages was to occupy myself with a definite task, so necessary in the long solitudes of gaol life, as well as to review past events in India, with which I had been connected, to enable myself to think clearly about them. I began the task in a mood of self- questioning and, to a large extent, this persisted throughout. ...
>
> My attempt was to trace, as far as I could, my own mental development, and not to write a survey of recent Indian history.

The Discovery of India was written in Ahmednagar Fort in 1944. It is a book of history and as Chalapathi Rau, the veteran journalist and Nehru's biographer puts it, 'There is much delving in the past and the present is traced to it, emphasizing the continuity.'

Glimpses of World History, originally written in the form of letters to his daughter, Indira Gandhi, is an analysis of the history of the world. It combines understanding with conviction, and impartiality with an outlook of high integrity. This is the first history of the world by a historical writer of a country subject to colonialism and deserves special attention.

Letters from a Father to his Daughter, again, is a compilation of a series of letters written to Indira Gandhi. In the words of the author : They were personal letters addressed to a little girl, ten years of age... I hope that such of them as read these letters may gradually begin to think of this world of ours as a large family of nations.

Letters from a Father to his Daughter, when published in book form had a 'generous reception'. It may remind one of H. G. Wells's *Outline of History*.

Besides these books, Nehru wrote innumerable letters, prefaces, memoranda and resolutions, and made speeches and statements incessantly. All these have been published.

Nehru's works (books, letters, collected speeches etc.) are important in themselves and need not always be read as an aid to the understanding of the mind of a great leader and statesman. These reveal his multifaceted personality and wide range of interests. A scientist by training and a student of history by choice, Nehru had love for aviation, adventure, wildlife and poetry. Clarity of thinking and clarity of expression are the two hallmarks of all his works. He avoids pomposity, shoddiness and cliches, and prefers freedom from artifice, smoothness of syntax and simplicity of diction. He was at his best when he was under emotional stress. There is a pattern and rhythm in all his writings and speeches and though he is not known to have attempted writing poetry, the poet hiding in him shows himself again and again in his works.

Selections from Nehru is so designed as to bring together, within a hundred odd pages, something of everything that Nehru wrote about. Nehru's own account of his childhood, the education he received in England, adventure in youth, love for animals, his views on education, economy, journalism, women's progress, the role of the developing country in the international arena—these are some of the themes of the pieces included in this book. It is believed that the readers of this volume will not only be acquainted with some of the important ideas and views of Nehru, but also recognize the distinct and unique style of Nehru's prose. If this slender volume can arouse the interest of the readers to study Nehru in greater detail, the purpose of preparing this work would be deemed a success.

Ganeswar Mishra
Sarat Chandra Satapathy

CHAPTER 1

CHILDHOOD

MY childhood was a sheltered and uneventful one. I listened to the grown-up talk of my cousins without always understanding all of it. Often this talk related to the overbearing character and insulting manners of the English people, as well as Eurasians, towards Indians, and how it was the duty of every Indian to stand up to this and not to tolerate it. Instances of conflicts between the rulers and the ruled were common and were fully discussed. It was a notorious fact that whenever an Englishman killed an Indian he was acquitted by a jury of his own countrymen. In railway trains compartments were reserved for Europeans and however crowded the train might be — and they used to be terribly crowded — no Indian was allowed to travel in them, even though they were empty. Even an unreserved compartment would be taken possession of by an Englishman and he would not allow any Indian to enter it. Benches and chairs were also reserved for Europeans in public parks and other places. I was filled with resentment against the alien rulers of my country who misbehaved in this manner, and whenever an Indian hit back I was glad. Not infrequently one of my cousins or one of their friends became personally involved in these individual encounters and then of course we all got very excited over it. One of the cousins was the strong man of the family and he loved to pick a quarrel with an Englishman, or more frequently with Eurasians, who, perhaps to show off their oneness with the ruling race, were often even more offensive than the English official or merchant. Such quarrels took place especially during railway journeys.

Much as I began to resent the presence and behaviour of the alien rulers, I had no feeling whatever, so far as I can remember, against individual Englishmen. I had had English governesses and occasionally I saw English friends of my father's visiting him. In my heart I rather admired the English.

In the evenings usually many friends came to visit father and he would relax after the tension of the day and the house would resound with his tremendous laughter. His laugh became famous in Allahabad. Sometimes I would peep at him and his friends from behind a curtain trying to make out what these great big people said to each other. If I was caught in the act I would be dragged out and, rather frightened, made to sit for a while on father's knee. Once I saw him drinking claret or some other red wine. Whisky I knew. I had often seen him and his friends drink it. But the new red stuff filled me with horror and I rushed to my mother to tell her that father was drinking blood.

I admired father tremendously. He seemed to me the embodiment of strength and courage and cleverness, far above all the other men I saw, and I treasured the hope that when I grew up I would be rather like him. But much as I admired him and loyed him I feared him also. I had seen him losing his temper at servants and others and he seemed to me terrible then and I shivered with fright, mixed sometimes with resentment, at the treatment of a servant. His temper was indeed an awful thing and even in after years I do not think I ever came across anything to match it in its own line. But, fortunately, he had a strong sense of humour also and an iron will, and he could control himself as a rule. As he grew older this power of control grew and it was very rare for him to indulge in anything like his old temper.

One of my earliest recollections is of this temper, for I was the victim of it. I must have been about five or six then. I noticed one day two fountain-pens on his office table and I looked at them with greed. I argued with myself that father could not require both at the same time and so I helped myself to one of them. Later I found that a mighty search was being made for the lost pen and I grew frightened at what I had done, but I did not confess. The pen was discovered and my guilt proclaimed to the world. Father was very angry and he gave me a tremendous thrashing. Almost blind with pain and mortification at my disgrace I rushed to mother, and for several days various creams and ointments were applied to my aching and quivering little body.

I do not remember bearing any ill-will towards my father because of this punishment. I think I must have felt that it was a just punishment, though perhaps overdone. But though my admiration and affection for him remained as strong as ever, fear formed a part of them. Not so with my mother. I had no fear of her, for I knew that she would condone everything I did, and, because of her excessive and indiscriminating love for me, I tried to dominate over her a little. I saw much more of her than I did of father and she seemed nearer to me and I would confide in her when I would not dream of doing so to father. She was *petite* and short of stature and soon I was almost as tall as she was and felt more of an equal with her. I admired her beauty and loved her amazingly small and beautiful hands and feet. She belonged to a fresher stock from Kashmir and her people had only left the homeland two generations back.

Another of my early confidants was a munshi of my father's, Munshi Mubarak Ali. He came from a well-to-do family of Badaun. The Revolt of 1857 had ruined the family and the English troops had partly exterminated it. This affliction had made him gentle and forbearing with everybody, especially with children, and for me he was a sure haven of refuge whenever I was unhappy or in touble. With his fine grey beard he seemed to my young eyes very ancient and full of old-time lore, and I used to snuggle up to him and listen, wide-eyed, by the hour to his innumerable stories—old tales from the *Arabian Nights* or other sources, or accounts of the happenings in 1857 and 1858. It was many years later, when I was grown up, that 'Munshiji' died, and the memory of him still remains with me as a dear and precious possession.

There were other stories also that I listened to, stories from the old Hindu mythology, from the epics, the *Ramayana* and the *Mahabharata*, that my mother and aunt used to tell us. My aunt, the widow of Pandit Nand Lal, was learned in the old Indian books and had an inexhaustible supply of these tales, and my knowledge of Indian mythology and folklore became quite considerable.

Of religion I had very hazy notions. It seemed to be a woman's affair. Father and my older cousins treated the question humorously and refused to take it seriously. The women of the family indulged in various ceremonies and *pujas* from time to time and I rather enjoyed them, though I tried to imitate to some extent the casual attitude of the grown-up men of the family. Sometimes I accompanied my mother or aunt to the Ganges for a dip, sometimes we visited temples in Allahabad itself or in Benares or elsewhere, or went to see a *sanyasi* reputed to be very holy. But all this left little impression on my mind.

Then there were the great festival days—the *Holi*, when all over the city there was a spirit of revelry and we could squirt water at each other; the *Divali*, the festival of light, when all the houses were lit up with thousands of dim lights in earthen cups; the *Janmashtami* to celebrate the birth, in prison, of Krishna at the midnight hour (but it was very difficult for us to keep awake till then); the *Dasehra* and *Ram Lila* when tableaux and processions re-enacted the old story of Ramachandra and his conquest of Lanka and vast crowds assembled to see them. All the children also went to see the Mohurrum processions with their silken *alums* and their sorrowful celebration of the tragic story of Hasan and Husain in distant Arabia. And on the two *Id* days Munshiji would dress up in his best attire and go to the big mosque for prayers, and I would go to his house and consume sweet vermicelli and other dainties. And then there were the smaller festivals of which there are many in the Hindu calendar. *Rakshabandhan, Bhayya duj,* etc.

Amongst us and the other Kashmiris there were also some special celebrations which were not observed by most of the other Hindus. Chief of these was the *Naoroz*, the New Year's Day according to the Samvat calendar. This was always a special day for us when all of us wore new clothes, and the young people of the house got small sums of money as tips.

But more than all these festivals I was interested in one annual event in which I played the central part—the celebration of the anniversary of my birth. This was a day of great excitement for me. Early in the morning I was weighed in a huge balance against some bagfuls of wheat and other articles which were then distributed to the poor; and then I arrayed myself in new clothes and received presents, and later in the day there was a party. I felt the hero of the occasion. My chief grievance was that my birthday came so rarely. Indeed I tried to start an agitation for more frequent birthdays. I did not realize then that a time would come when birthdays would become unpleasant reminders of advancing age.

Sometimes the whole family journeyed to a distant town to attend a marriage, either of a cousin of mine or of some more distant relation or friend. Those were exciting journeys for us children, for all rules were relaxed during these marriage festivities and we had the free run of the place. Numerous families usually lived crowded together in the *shadi-khana*, the marriage house, where the party stayed, and there were many boys and girls and children. On these occasions I could not complain of loneliness and we had our heart's fill of play and mischief, with an occasional scolding from our elders.

Indian marriages, both among the rich and the poor, have had their full share of condemnation as wasteful and extravagant display. They deserve all this. Even apart from the waste, it is most painful to see the vulgar display which has no artistic or aesthetic value of any kind. (Needless to say there are exceptions.) For all this the really guilty people are the middle classes. The poor are also extravagant, even at the cost of burdensome debts, but it is the height of absurdity to say, as some people do, that their poverty is due to their social customs. It is often forgotten that the life of the poor is terribly dull and monotonous, and an occasional marriage celebration, bringing with it some feasting and singing, comes to them as an oasis in a desert of soulless toil, a refuge from domesticity and the prosaic business of life. Who would be cruel enough to deny this consolation to them, who have such few occasions for laughter ? Stop waste by all means, lessen the extravagance (big and foolish words to use for the little show that the poor put up in their poverty!), but do not make their life more drab and cheerless than it is.

So also for the middle classes. Waste and extravagance apart these marriages are big social reunions where distant relations and old friends meet after long intervals. India is a big country and it is not easy for friends to meet, and for many to meet together at the same time is still more difficult. Hence the popularity of the marriage celebrations. The only rival to them, and it has already excelled them in many ways even as a social reunion, is the political gathering, the various conferences, or the Congress !

Kashmiris have had one advantage over many others in India, especially in the north. They have never had any purdah, or seclusion of women, among themselves. Finding this custom prevailing in the Indian plains, when they came down, they adopted it, but only partly and in so far as their relations with others and non-Kashmiris were concerned. That was considered then in northern India, where most of the Kashmiris stayed, an inevitable sign of social status. But among themselves they stuck to the free social life of men and women, and every Kashmiri had the free *entree* into any Kashmiri house. In Kashmiri feasts and ceremonies men and women met together and sat together, though often the women would sit in one bunch. Boys and girls used to meet on a more or less equal footing. They did not, of course, have the freedom of the modern West.

So passed my early years. Sometimes, as was inevitable in a large family, there were family squabbles. When these happened to assume unusual proportions they reached my father's ears and he was angry and seemed to think that all such happenings were due to the folly of women. I did not understand what exactly had happened but I saw that something was very wrong as people seemed to speak in a peculiarly disagreeable way or to avoid each other. I felt very unhappy. Father's intervention, when it took place, shook us all up.

One little incident of those early days stands out in my memory. I must have been about seven or eight then. I used to go out every day for a ride accompanied by a *sawar* from a cavalry unit then stationed in Allahabad. One evening I had a fall and my pony—a pretty animal, partly Arab—returned home without me. Father was giving a tennis party. There was great consternation and all the members of the party, headed by father, formed a procession in all kinds of vehicles, and set out in search of me. They met me on the way and I was treated as if I had performed some heroic deed !

An Autobiography, 1936, pp. 6-11

CHAPTER 2
HARROW

ON a May day, towards the end of the month, we reached London, reading in the train from Dover of the great Japanese sea victory at Tsushima. I was in high good humour. The very next day happened to be Derby day and we went to see the race. I remember meeting, soon after our arrival in London, M.A. Ansari, who was then a smart and clever young man with a record of brilliant academical achievement behind him. He was a house surgeon at the time in a London hospital.

I was a little fortunate in finding a vacancy at Harrow for I was slightly above the usual age for entry, being fifteen. My family went to the Continent and after some months they returned to India.

Never before had I been left among strangers all by myself and I felt lonely and homesick, but not for long. I managed to fit in to some extent in the life at school and work and play kept me busy. I was never an exact fit. Always I had a feeling that I was not one of them, and the others must have felt the same way about me. I was left a little to myself. But on the whole I took my full share in the games, without in any way shining at them, and it was, I believe, recognized that I was no shirker.

I was put, to begin with, in a low form because of my small knowledge of Latin, but I was pushed higher up soon. In many subjects probably, and especially in general knowledge, I was in advance of those of my age. My interests were certainly wider, and I read both books and newspapers more than most of my fellow-students. I remember writing to my father how dull most of the English boys were as they could talk about nothing but their games. But there were exceptions, especially when I reached the upper forms.

I was greatly interested in the General Election, which took place, as far as I remember, at the end of 1905 and which ended in a great Liberal victory. Early in 1906 our form master asked us about the new Government and, much to his surprise, I was the only boy in his form who could give him much information on the subject, including almost a complete list of members of Campbell-Bannerman's Cabinet.

Apart from politics another subject that fascinated me was the early growth of aviation. Those were the days of the Wright Brothers and Santos Dumont (to be followed soon by Farman, Latham and Blériot), and I wrote to father from Harrow, in my enthusiasm, that soon I might be able to pay him a week-end visit in India by air.

There were four or five Indian boys at Harrow in my time. I seldom came across those at other houses, but in our own house — the Headmaster's — we had one of the sons of the Gaekwar of Baroda. He was much senior to me and was popular because of his cricket. He left soon after my arrival. Later came the eldest son of the Maharaja of Kapurthala Paramjit Singh, now the Tikka Sahab. He was a complete misfit and was unhappy and could not mix at all with the other boys, who often made fun of him and his ways. This irritated him greatly and sometimes he used to tell them what he would do to them if they came to Kapurthala. Needless to say, this did not improve matters for him. He had previously spent some time in France and could speak French fluently but, oddly enough, such were the methods of teaching foreign languages in English public schools, that this hardly helped him in the French classes.

A curious incident took place once when, in the middle of the night, the house-master suddenly visited our rooms and made a thorough search all over the house. We learnt that Paramjit Singh had lost his beautiful gold-mounted cane. The search was not successful. Two or three days later the Eton and Harrow match took place at Lord's, and immediately afterwards the cane was discovered in the owner's room. Evidently some one had used it at Lord's and then returned it.

There were a few Jews in our house and in other houses. They got on fairly well but there was always a background of anti-Semitic feeling. They were the 'damned Jews', and soon, almost unconsciously, I began to think that it was the proper thing to have this feeling. I never really felt anti-Semitic in the least, and, in later years, I had many good friends among the Jews.

I got used to Harrow and liked the place, and yet somehow I began to feel that I was outgrowing it. The university attracted me.

Right through the years 1906 and 1907 news from India had been agitating me. I got meagre enough accounts from the English papers; but even that little showed that big events were happening at home, in Bengal, Punjab, and the Maharashtra. There was Lala Lajpat Rai's and S. Ajit Singh's deportation, and Bengal seemed to be in an uproar, and Tilak's name was often flashed from Poona, and there was Swadeshi and boycott. All this stirred me tremendously; but there was not a soul in Harrow to whom I could talk about it. During the holidays I met some of my cousins or other Indian friends and then had a chance of relieving my mind.

A prize I got for good work at school was one of G. M. Trevelyan's Garibaldi books. This fascinated me and soon I obtained the other two volumes of the series and studied the whole Garibaldi story in them carefully. Visions of similar deeds in India came before me, of a gallant fight for freedom, and in my mind India and Italy got strangely mixed together. Harrow seemed a rather small and restricted place for these ideas and I wanted to go to the wider sphere of the university. So I induced father to agree to this and left Harrow after only two years' stay, which was much less than the usual period.

I was leaving Harrow because I wanted to do so myself and yet, I well remember, that when the time came to part I felt unhappy and tears came to my eyes. I had grown rather fond of the place and my departure for good put an end to one period in my life. And yet, I wonder, how far I was really sorry at leaving Harrow. Was it not partly a feeling that I ought to be unhappy because Harrow tradition and song demanded it ? I was susceptible to these traditions for I had deliberately not resisted them so as to be in harmony with the place.

An Autobiography, 1936, pp. 17-19

CHAPTER 3

AN ADVENTURE IN THE HIMALAYAS

IN the summer of 1916 we spent some months in Kashmir. I left my family in the valley and, together with a cousin of mine, wandered for several weeks in the mountains and went up the Ladakh road.

This was my first experience of the narrow and lonely valleys, high up in the world, which lead to the Tibetan plateau. From the top of the Zoji-la pass we saw the rich verdant mountain sides below us on one side and the bare bleak rock on the other. We went up and up the narrow valley bottom flanked on each side by mountains, with the snow-covered tops gleaming on one side and little glaciers creeping down to meet us. The wind was cold and bitter but the sun was warm in the day time, and the air was so clear that often we were misled about the distance of objects, thinking them much nearer than they actually were. The loneliness grew; there were not even trees or vegetation to keep us company—only the bare rock and the snow and ice and, sometimes, very welcome flowers. Yet I found a strange satisfaction in these wild and desolate haunts of nature; I was full of energy and a feeling of exaltation.

I had an exciting experience during this visit. At one place on our march beyond the Zoji-la pass—I think it was called Matayan—we were told that the cave of Amaranath was only eight miles away. It was true that an enormous mountain all covered with ice and snow lay in between and had to be crossed, but what did that matter? Eight miles seemed so little. In our enthusiasm and inexperience we decided to make the attempt. So we left our camp (which was situated at about 11,500 feet altitude) and with a small party went up the mountain. We had a local shepherd for a guide.

We crossed and climbed several glaciers, roping ourselves up, and our troubles increased and breathing became a little difficult. Some of our porters, lightly laden as they were, began to bring up blood. It began to snow and the glaciers became terribly slippery: we were fagged out and every step meant a special effort. But still we persisted in our foolhardy attempt. We had left our camp at four in the morning and after twelve hours' almost continous climbing we were rewarded by the sight of a huge ice-field. This was a magnificent sight, surrounded as it was by snow-peaks, like a diadem or an amphitheatre of the gods. But fresh snow and mists soon hid the sight from us. I do not know what our altitude was but I think it must have been about 15,000 to 16,000 feet, as we were considerably higher than the cave of Amaranath. We had now to cross this ice-field, a distance probably of half a mile, and then go down on the other side to the cave. We thought that as the climbing was over, our principal difficulties had also been surmounted, and so, very tired but in good humour, we began this stage of the journey. It was a tricky business as there were many crevasses and the fresh snow often covered a dangerous spot. It was this fresh snow that almost proved to be my undoing, for I stepped upon it and it gave way and down I went a huge and yawning crevasse. It was a tremendous fissure and anything that went right down it could be assured of safe keeping and preservation for some geological ages. But the rope held and I clutched to the side of the crevasse and was pulled out. We were shaken up by this but still we persisted in going on. The crevasses, however, increased in number and width and we had no equipment or means of crossing some of them. And so at last we turned back, weary and disappointed, and the cave of Amaranath remained unvisited.

The higher valleys and mountains of Kashmir fascinated me so much that I resolved to come back again soon. I made many a plan and worked out many a tour, and one, the very thought of which filled me with delight, was a visit to Manasarovar, the wonder lake of Tibet, and snow-covered Kailas near by. That was eighteen years ago, and I am still as far as ever from Kailas and Manasarovar. I have not even been to visit Kashmir again, much as I have longed to, and ever more and more I have got entangled in the coils of politics and public affairs. Instead of going up mountains or crossing the seas I have to satisfy my wanderlust by coming to prison, and besides what else can one do in prison? And I dream of the day when I shall wander about the Himalayas and cross them to reach that lake and mountain of my desire. But meanwhile the sands of life run on and youth passes into middle age and that will give place to something worse, and sometimes I think that I may grow too old to reach Kailas and Manasarovar. But the journey is always worth the making even though the end may not be in sight.

> Yea, in my mind these mountains rise,
>   Their perils dyed with evening's rose;
> And still my ghost sits at my eyes
>   And thirsts for their untroubled snows.

– Walter de la Mare

An Autobiography, 1936, pp. 37-39

CHAPTER 4

ANIMALS IN PRISON

FOR fourteen and a half months I lived in my little cell or room in the Dehra Dun Gaol, and I began to feel as if I was almost a part of it. I was familiar with every bit of it; I knew every mark and dent on the whitewashed walls and on the uneven floor and the ceiling with its moth-eaten rafters. In the little yard outside I greeted little tufts of grass and odd bits of stone as old friends. I was not alone in my cell, for several colonies of wasps and hornets lived there, and many lizards found a home behind the rafters, emerging in the evenings in search of prey. If thoughts and emotions leave their traces behind in the physical surroundings, the very air of that cell must be thick with them, and they must cling to every object in that little space.

.I had had better cells in other prisons, but in Dehra Dun I had one privilege which was very precious to me. The gaol proper was a very small one, and we were kept in an old lock-up outside the gaol walls, but within the gaol compound. This place was so small that there was no room to walk about in it, and so we were allowed, morning and evening, to go out and walk up and down in front of the gate, a distance of about a hundred yards. We remained in the gaol compound, but this coming outside the walls gave us a view of the mountains and the fields and a public road at some distance. This was not a special privilege for me; it was common for all the A and B Class prisoners kept at Dehra Dun. Within the compound, but outside the gaol walls, there was another small building called the European Lock-up. This had no enclosing wall, and a person inside the cell could have a fine view of the mountains and the life outside. European convicts and others kept here were also allowed to walk in front of the gaol gate every morning and evening.

Only a prisoner who has been confined for long behind high walls can appreciate the extraordinary psychological value of these outside walks and open views. I loved these outings, and I did not give them up even during the monsoon, when the rain came down for days in torrents and I had to walk in ankle-deep of water. I would have welcomed the outing in any place, but the sight of the towering Himalayas near by was an added joy which went a long way to removing the weariness of prison. It was my good fortune that during the long period when I had no interviews, and when for many months I was quite alone, I could gaze at these mountains that I loved. I could not see the mountains from my cell, but my mind was full of them and I was ever conscious of their nearness, and a secret intimacy seemed to grow between us.

> Flocks of birds have flown high and away;
> A solitary drift of cloud, too, has gone, wandering on
> And I sit along with Ching-ting Peak, towering beyond.
> We never grow tired of each other, the mountain and I.

I am afraid I cannot say with the poet, Li T'ai Po, that I never grew weary, even of the mountain; but that was a rare experience, and, as a rule, I found great comfort in its proximity. Its solidity and imperturbability looked down upon me with the wisdom of a million years, and mocked at my varying humours and soothed my fevered mind.

Spring was very pleasant in Dehra, and it was a far longer one than in the plains below. The winter had denuded almost all the trees of their leaves, and they stood naked and bare. Even four magnificent peepal trees, which stood in front of the gaol gate, much to my surprise, dropped nearly all their leaves. Gaunt and cheerless they stood there, till the spring air warmed them up again and sent a message of life to their innermost cells. Suddenly there was a stir both in the peepals and the other trees, and an air of mystery surrounded them as of secret operations going on behind the scenes; and I would be startled to find little bits of green peeping out all over them. It was a gay and cheering sight. And then, very rapidly, the leaves would come out in their millions and glisten in the sunlight and play about in the breeze. How wonderful is the sudden change from bud to leaf!

I had never noticed before that fresh mango leaves are reddish-brown, russet coloured, remarkably like the autumn tints on the Kashmir hills. But they change colour soon and become green.

The monsoon rains were always welcome, for they ended the

summer heat. But one could have too much of a good thing, and Dehra Dun is one of the favoured haunts of the rain god. Within the first five or six weeks of the break of the monsoon we would have about fifty or sixty inches of rain, and it was not pleasant to sit cooped up in a little narrow place trying to avoid the water dripping from the ceiling or rushing in from the windows.

Autumn again was pleasant, and so was the winter, except when it rained. With thunder and rain and piercing cold winds, one longed for a decent habitation and a little warmth and comfort. Occasionally there would be a hailstorm, with hailstones bigger than marbles coming down on the corrugated iron roofs and making a tremendous noise, something like an artillery bombardment.

I remember one day particularly; it was the 24th of December, 1932. There was a thunderstorm and rain all day, and it was bitterly cold. Altogether it was one of the most miserable days, from the bodily point of view, that I have spent in gaol. In the evening it cleared up suddenly, and all my misery departed when I saw all the neighbouring mountains and hills covered with a thick mantle of snow. The next day—Christmas Day—was lovely and clear, and there was a beautiful view of snow-covered mountains.

Prevented from indulging in normal activities we became more observant of nature's ways. We watched also the various animals and insects that came our way. As I grew more observant I noticed all manner of insects living in my cell or in the little yard outside. I realized that while I complained of loneliness, that yard, which seemed empty and deserted, was teeming with life. All these creeping or crawling or flying insects lived their life without interfering with me in any way, and I saw no reason why I should interfere with them. But there was continuous war between me and bed-bugs, mosquitos, and, to some extent, flies. Wasps and hornets I tolerated, and there were hundreds of them in my cell. There had been a little tiff between us when, inadvertently I think, a wasp had stung me. In my anger I tried to exterminate the lot, but they put up a brave fight in defence of their temporary home, which probably contained their eggs, and I desisted and decided to leave them in peace if they did not interfere with me any more. For over a year after that I lived in that cell surrounded by these wasps and hornets, and they never attacked me, and we respected each other.

Bats I did not like, but I had to endure them. They flew soundlessly in the evening dusk, and one could just see them against the darkening sky. Eerie things; I had a horror of them. They seemed to pass within an inch of one's face, and I was always afraid that they might hit me. Higher up in the air passed the big bats, the flying foxes.

I used to watch the ants and the white ants and other insects by the hour. And the lizards as they crept about in the evenings and stalked their prey and chased each other, wagging their tails in a most comic fashion. Ordinarily they avoided wasps, but twice I saw them stalk them with enormous care and seize them from the front. I do not know if this avoidance of the sting was intentional or accidental.

Then there were squirrels, crowds of them if trees were about. They would become very venturesome and come right near us. In Lucknow Gaol I used to sit reading almost without moving for considerable periods, and a squirrel would climb up my leg and sit on my knee and have a look round. And then it would look into my eyes and realize that I was not a tree or whatever it had taken me for. Fear would disable it for a moment, and then it would scamper away. Little baby squirrels would sometimes fall down from the trees. The mother would come after them, roll them up into a little ball, and carry them off to safety. Occasionally the baby got lost. One of my companions picked up three of these lost baby squirrels and looked after them. They were so tiny that it was a problem how to feed them. The problem was, however, solved rather ingeniously. A fountain-pen filler, with a little cotton wool attached to it, made an efficient feeding bottle.

Pigeons abounded in all the gaols I went to, except in the mountain prison of Almora. There were thousands of them, and in the evenings the sky would be thick with them. Sometimes the gaol officials would shoot them down and feed on them. There were mainas, of course; they are to be found everywhere. A pair of them nested over my cell door in Dehra Dun, and I used to feed them. They grew quite tame, and if there was any delay in their morning or evening meal they would sit quite near me and loudly demand their food. It was amusing to watch their signs and listen to their impatient cries.

In Naini there were thousands of parrots, and large numbers of them lived in the crevices of my barrack walls. Their courtship and love-making was always a fascinating sight, and sometimes there were fierce quarrels between two male parrots over a lady parrot, who sat calmly by waiting for the result of the encounter and ready to grant her favours to the winner.

Dehra Dun had a variety of birds, and there was a regular jumble of singing and lively chattering and twittering, and high above it all came the koël's plaintive call. During the monsoon and just before it the Brain-Fever bird visited us, and I realized soon why it was so named. It was amazing the persistence with which it went on repeating the same notes, in daytime and at night, in sunshine and in pouring rain. We could not see most of these birds, we could only hear them as a rule, as there were no trees in our little yard. But I used to watch the eagles and the kites gliding gracefully high up in the air, sometimes swooping down and then allowing themselves to be carried up by a current of air. Often a horde of wild duck would fly over our heads.

There was a large colony of monkeys in Bareilly Gaol and their antics were always worth watching. One incident impressed me. A baby monkey managed to come down into our barrack enclosure and he could not mount up the wall again. The warder and some convict overseers and other prisoners caught hold of him and tied a bit of string round his neck. The parents (presumably) of the little one saw all this from the top of the high wall, and their anger grew. Suddenly one of them, a huge monkey, jumped down and charged almost right into the crowd which surrounded the baby monkey. It was an extraordinary brave thing to do, for the warder and C.O.'s had sticks and *lathis* and they were brandishing them about, and there was quite a crowd of them. Reckless courage triumphed, and the crowd of humans fled, terrified, leaving their sticks behind them! The little monkey was rescued.

We had often animal visitors that were not welcome. Scorpions were frequently found in our cells, especially after a thunderstorm. It was surprising that I was never stung by one, for I would come across them in the most unlikely places—on my bed, or sitting on a book which I had just lifted up. I kept a particularly black and poisonous-looking brute in a bottle for some time, feeding him with flies, etc., and then when I tied him up on a wall with a string he managed to escape. I had no desire to meet him loose again, and so I cleaned my cell out and hunted for him everywhere, but he had vanished.

Three or four snakes were also found in my cells or near them. News of one of them got out, and there were headlines in the Press. As a matter of fact I welcomed the diversion. Prison life is dull enough, and everything that breaks through the monotony is appreciated. Not that I appreciate or welcome snakes, but they do not fill me with terror as they do some people. I am afraid of their bite, of course, and would protect myself if I saw a snake. But there would be no feeling of repulsion or overwhelming fright. Centipedes horrify me much more: it is not so much fear as instinctive repulsion. In Alipore Gaol in Calcutta I woke in the middle of the night and felt something crawling over my foot. I pressed a torch I had and I saw a centipede on the bed. Instinctively and with amazing rapidity I vaulted clear out of that bed and nearly hit the cell wall. I realized fully then what Pavlov's reflexes were.

In Dehra Dun I saw a new animal, or rather an animal which was new to me. I was standing at the gaol gate talking to the gaoler when we noticed a man outside carrying a strange animal. The gaoler sent for him, and I saw something between a lizard and a crocodile, about two feet long with claws and a scaly covering. This uncouth animal, which was very much alive, had been twisted round in a most peculiar way forming a kind of knot, and its owner had passed a pole through this knot and was merrily carrying it in this fashion. He called it a 'Bo'. When asked by the gaoler what he proposed to do with it, he replied with a broad smile that he would make *bhujji*—a kind of curry—out of it! He was a forest-dweller. Subsequently I discovered from reading F. W. Champion's book—*The Jungle in Sunlight and Shadow*—that this animal was the Pangolin.

Prisoners, especially long-term convicts, have to suffer most from emotional starvation. Often they seek some emotional satisfaction by keeping animal pets. The ordinary prisoner cannot keep them, but the convict overseers have a little more freedom and the gaol staff usually does not object. The commonest pets were squirrels and, strangely, mongooses. Dogs are not allowed in gaols, but cats seem to be encouraged. A little kitten made friends with me once. It belonged to a gaol official, and when he was transferred he took it away with him. I missed it. Although dogs are not allowed, I got tied up with some dogs accidentally in Dehra Dun. A gaol official had brought a bitch, and then he was transferred, and he deserted her. The poor thing became a homeless wanderer, living under culverts, picking up scraps from the warders, usually starving. As I was being kept in the lock-up outside the gaol proper, she used to come to me begging for food. I began to feed her regularly, and she gave birth to a litter of pups under a culvert. Many of these were taken away, but three remained and I fed them. One of the puppies fell ill with a violent distemper, and gave me a great deal of trouble. I nursed her with care, and sometimes I would get up a dozen times in the course of the night to look after her. She survived, and I was happy that my nursing had pulled her round.

I came in contact with animals far more in prison than I had done outside. I had always been fond of dogs, and had kept some, but I could never look after them properly as other matters claimed my attention. In prison I was grateful for their company. Indians do not, as a rule, approve of animals as household pets. It is remarkable that in spite of their general philosophy of non-violence to animals, they are often singularly careless and unkind to them. Even the cow, that favoured animal, though looked up to and almost worshipped by many Hindus and often the cause of riots, is not treated kindly. Worship and kindliness do not always go together.

Different countries have adopted different animals as symbols of their ambition or character—the eagle of the United States of America and of Germany, the lion and bulldog of England, the fighting-cock of France, the bear of old Russia. How far do these patron animals mould national character? Most of them are aggressive, fighting animals, beasts of prey. It is not surprising that the people who grow up with these examples before them should mould themselves consciously after them and strike up aggressive attitudes, and roar, and prey on others. Nor is it surprising that the Hindu should be mild and non-violent, for his patron animal is the cow. *An Autobiography*, 1936, pp. 353-59

CHAPTER 5

LIFE'S PHILOSOPHY

SIX or seven years ago an American publisher asked me to write an essay on my philosophy of life for a symposium he was preparing. I was attracted to the idea but I hesitated, and the more I thought over it, the more reluctant I grew. Ultimately I did not write that essay.

What was my philosophy of life ? I did not know. Some years earlier I would not have been so hesitant. There was a definiteness about my thinking and objectives then which has faded away since. The events of the past few years in India, China, Europe, and all over the world have been confusing, upsetting and distressing, and the future has become vague and shadowy and has lost that clearness of outline which it once possessed in my mind.

This doubt and difficulty about fundamental matters did not come in my way in regard to immediate action, except that it blunted somewhat the sharp edge of that activity. No longer could I function, as I did in my younger days, as an arrow flying automatically to the target of my choice, ignoring all else but that target. Yet I functioned, for the urge to action was there and a real or imagined co-ordination of that action with the ideals I held. But a growing distaste for politics, as I saw them, seized me and gradually my whole attitude to life seemed to undergo a transformation.

The ideals and objectives of yesterday were still the ideals of today but they had lost some of their lustre, and even as one seemed to go towards them, they lost the shining beauty which had warmed the heart and vitalized the body. Evil triumphed often enough, but what was far worse was the coarsening and distortion of what had seemed so right. Was human nature so essentially bad that it would take ages of training, through suffering and misfortune, before it could behave reasonably and raise man above that creature of lust and violence and deceit that he now was? And meanwhile was every effort to change it radically in the present or the near future doomed to failure ?

Ends and means: were they tied up inseparably, acting and reacting on each other, the wrong means distorting and sometimes even destroying the end in view ? But the right means might well be beyond the capacity of infirm and selfish human nature. What then was one to do ? Not to act was a complete confession of failure and a submission to evil; to act meant often enough a compromise with some form of that evil, with all the untoward consequences that such compromises result in.

My early approach to life's problems had been more or less scientific, with something of the easy optimism of the science of the nineteenth and early twentieth century. A secure and comfortable existence, and the energy and self-confidence I possessed, increased that feeling of optimism. A kind of vague humanism appealed to me.

Religion, as I saw it practised, and accepted even by thinking minds, whether it was Hinduism, or Islam, or Buddhism, or Christianity, did not attract me. It seemed to be closely associated with superstitious practices and dogmatic beliefs, and behind it lay a method of approach to life's problems which was certainly not that of science. There was an element of magic about it, an uncritical credulousness, a reliance on the supernatural.

Yet it was obvious that religion had supplied some deeply felt inner need of human nature, and that the vast majority of people all over the world could not do without some form of religious belief. It had produced many fine types of men and women, as well as bigoted, narrow-minded, cruel tyrants. It had given a set of values to human life, and though some of these values had no application today, or were even harmful, others were still the foundation of morality and ethics.

In the wider sense of the word, religion dealt with the uncharted regions of human experience, uncharted, that is, by the scientific positive knowledge of the day. In a sense it might be considered an extension of the known and charted region, though the methods of science and religion were utterly unlike each other, and to a large extent they had to deal with different kinds of media. It was obvious that there was a vast unknown region all around us and science, with its magnificent achievements, knew little enough about it, though it was making tentative approaches in that direction. Probably also the normal methods of science, its dealings with the visible world and the processes of life, were not wholly adapted to the psychical, the artistic, the spiritual, and other elements of the invisible world which is undergoing change in time and space. It is continually touching an invisible world of other, and possibly more stable or equally changeable elements, and no thinking person can ignore this invisible world.

Science does not tell us much, or for the matter of that anything, about the purpose of life. It is now widening its boundaries and it may invade the so-called invisible world before long and help us to understand this purpose of life in its widest sense, or at least give us some glimpses which illumine the problem of human existence. The old controversy between science and religion takes a new form—the application of the scientific method to emotional and religious experiences.

Religion merges into mysticism and metaphysics and philosophy. There have been great mystics, attractive figures, who cannot easily be disposed of as self-deluded fools. Yet mysticism (in the narrow sense of the word) irritates me; it appears to be vague and soft and flabby, not a rigorous discipline of the mind but a surrender of mental faculties and a living in a sea of emotional experience. The experience may lead occasionally to some insight into inner and less obvious processes, but it is also likely to lead to self-delusion.

Metaphysics and philosophy, or a metaphysical philosophy, have a greater appeal to the mind. They require hard thinking and the application of logic and reasoning, though all this is necessarily based on some premises, which are presumed to be self-evident, and yet which may or may not be true. All thinking persons, to a greater or less degree, dabble in metaphysics and philosophy, for not to do so is to ignore many of the aspects of this universe of ours. Some may feel more attracted to them than others, and the emphasis on them may vary in different ages. In the ancient world, both in Asia and Europe, all the emphasis was laid on the supremacy of the inward life over things external, and this inevitably led to metaphysics and philosophy. The modern man is wrapped up much more in these things external, and yet even he, in moments of crisis and mental trouble, often turns to philosophy and metaphysical speculations.

Some vague or more precise philosophy of life we all have, though most of us accept unthinkingly the general attitude which is characteristic of our generation and environment. Most of us accept also certain metaphysical conceptions as part of the faith in which we have grown up. I have not been attracted towards metaphysics; in fact I have had a certain distaste for vague speculation. And yet I have sometimes found a certain intellectual fascination in trying to follow the rigid lines of metaphysical and philosophic thought of the ancients or the moderns. But I have never felt at ease there and have escaped from their spell with a feeling of relief.

Essentially I am interested in this world, in this life, not in some other world or a future life. Whether there is such a thing as a soul, or whether there is a survival after death or not, I do not know; and, important as these questions are, they do not trouble me in the least. The environment in which I have grown up takes the soul (or rather the *atma*) and a future life, the *Karma* theory of cause and effect, and re-incarnation for granted. I have been affected by this and so, in a sense, I am favourably disposed towards these assumptions. There might be a soul which survives the physical death of the body, and a theory of cause and effect governing life's actions seems reasonable though it leads to obvious difficulties when one thinks of the ultimate cause. Presuming a soul, there appears to be some logic also in the theory of re-incarnation.

But I do not believe in any of these or other theories and assumptions as a matter of religious faith. They are just intellectual speculations in an unknown region about which we know next to nothing. They do not affect my life, and whether they were proved right or wrong subsequently, they would make little difference to me.

Spiritualism with its seances and its so-called manifestations of spirits and the like has always seemed to me a rather absurd and impertinent way of investigating psychic phenomena and the mysteries of the after-life. Usually it is something worse and is an exploitation of the emotions of some over-credulous people who seek relief or escape from mental trouble. I do not deny the possibility of some of these psychic phenomena having a basis of truth, but the approach appears to me to be all wrong and the conclusions drawn from scraps and odd bits of evidence to be unjustified.

Often, as I look at this world, I have a sense of mysteries, of unknown depths. The urge to understand it, in so far as I can, comes to me; to be in tune with it and to experience it in its fullness. But the way to that understanding seems to me essentially the way of science, the way of objective approach, though I realize that there can be no such thing as true objectiveness. If the subjective element is unavoidable and inevitable, it should be conditioned as far as possible by the scientific method.

What the mysterious is I do not know. I do not call it God because God has come to mean much that I do not believe in. I find myself incapable of thinking of a deity or of any unknown supreme power in anthropomorphic terms, and the fact that many people think so is continually a source of surprise to me. Any idea of a personal God seems very odd to me. Intellectually, I can appreciate to some extent the conception of monism, and I have been attracted towards the *Advaita* (non-dualist) philosophy of the *Vedanta,* though I do not presume to understand it in all its depth and intricacy, and I realize that merely an intellectual appreciation of such matters does not carry one far. At the same time the *Vedanta,* as well as other similar approaches, rather frighten me with their vague formless incursions into infinity. The diversity and fullness of nature stir me and produce a harmony of the spirit, and I can imagine myself feeling at home in the old Indian or Greek pagan and pantheistic atmosphere, but minus the conception of god or gods that was attached to it.

Some kind of ethical approach to life has a strong appeal for me, though it would be difficult for me to justify it logically. I have been attracted by Gandhiji's stress on right means and I think one of his greatest contributions to our public life has been this emphasis. The idea is by no means new, but this application of an ethical doctrine to large-scale public activity was certainly novel. It is full of difficulty, and perhaps ends and means are not really separable and form together one organic whole. In a world which thinks almost exclusively of ends and ignores means, this emphasis on means seems odd and remarkable. How far it has succeeded in India I cannot say. But there is no doubt that it has created a deep and abiding impression on the minds of large numbers of people.

A study of Marx and Lenin produced a powerful effect on my mind and helped me to see history and current affairs in a new light. The long chain of history and of social development appeared to have some meaning, some sequence, and the future lost some of its obscurity. The practical achievements of the Soviet Union were also tremendously impressive. Often I disliked or did not understand some development there and it seemed to me to be too closely concerned with the opportunism of the moment or the power politics of the day. But despite all these developments and possible distortions of the original passion for human betterment, I had no doubt that the Soviet Revolution had advanced human society by a great leap and had lit a bright flame which could not be smothered, and that it had laid the foundations for that 'new civilization' towards which the world would advance. I am too much of an individualist and believer in personal freedom to like overmuch regimentation. Yet it seemed to me obvious that in a complex social structure individual freedom had to be limited, and perhaps the only way to real personal freedom was through some such limitation in the social sphere. The lesser liberties may often need limitation in the interest of the larger freedom.

Much in the Marxist philosophical outlook I could accept without difficulty: its monism and non-duality of mind and matter, the dynamics of matter and the dialectic of continuous change by evolution as well as leap, through action and interaction, cause and effect, thesis, antithesis and synthesis. It did not satisfy me completely, nor did it answer all the questions in my mind, and, almost unawares, a vague idealist approach would creep into my mind, something rather akin to the *Vedanta* approach. It was not a difference between mind and matter but rather of something that lay beyond the mind. Also there was the background of ethics. I realized that the moral approach is a changing one and depends upon the growing mind and an advancing civilization; it is conditioned by the mental climate of the age. Yet there was something more to it than that, certain basic urges which had greater permanence. I did not like the frequent divorce in communist, as in other practice, between action and these basic urges or principles. So there was an odd mixture in my mind which I could not rationally explain or resolve. There was a general tendency not to think too much of those fundamental questions which appear to be beyond reach, and rather to concentrate on the problems of life—to understand in the narrower and more immediate sense what should be done and how. Whatever ultimate reality may be, and whether we can ever grasp it in whole or in part, there certainly appear to be vast possibilities of increasing human knowledge, even though this may be partly or largely subjective, and of applying this to the advancement and betterment of human living and social organization.

There has been in the past, and there is to a lesser extent even today among some people, an absorption in finding an answer to the riddle of the universe. This leads them away from the individual and social problems of the day, and when they are unable to solve that riddle they despair and turn to inaction and triviality, or find comfort in some dogmatic creed. Social evils, most of which are certainly capable of removal, are attributed to original sin, to the unalterableness of 'human nature', or the social structure, or (in India) to the inevitable legacy of previous births. Thus one drifts away from even the attempt to think rationally and scientifically and takes refuge in irrationalism, superstition, and unreasonable and inequitable social prejudices and practices. It is true that even rational and scientific thought does not always take us as far as we would like to go. There is an infinite number of factors and relations which influence and determine events in varying degrees and it is impossible to grasp all of them. Still we can try to pick out the dominating forces at work and by observing external material reality, and by experiment and practice, trial and error, grope our way to ever-widening knowledge and truth.

For this purpose, and within these limitations, the general Marxist approach, fitting in as it more or less did with the present state of scientific knowledge, seemed to me to offer considerable help. But even accepting that approach, the consequences that flow from it and the interpretation on past and present happenings were by no means always clear. Marx's general analysis of social development seems to have been remarkably correct, and yet many developments took place later which did not fit in with his outlook for the immediate future. Lenin successfully adapted the Marxian thesis to some of these subsequent developments, and again since then further remarkable changes have taken place—the rise of fascism and nazism and all that lay behind them. The very rapid growth of technology and the practical application of vast developments in scientific knowledge are now changing the world picture with an amazing rapidity, leading to new problems.

And so while I accepted the fundamentals of the socialist theory, I did not trouble myself about its numerous inner controversies. I had little patience with leftist groups in India, spending much of their energy in mutual conflict and recrimination over fine points of doctrine which did not interest me at all. Life is too complicated and, as far as we can understand it in our present state of knowledge, too illogical for it to be confined within the four corners of a fixed doctrine.

The real problems for me remain problems of individual and social life, of harmonious living, of a proper balancing of an individual's inner and outer life, of an adjustment of the relations between individuals and between groups, of a continuous becoming something better and higher, of social development, of the ceaseless adventure of man. In the solution of these problems the way of observation and precise knowledge and deliberate reasoning, according to the method of science, must be followed. This method may not always be applicable in our quest of truth, for art and poetry and certain psychic experiences seem to belong to a different order of things and to elude the objective methods of science. Let us therefore not rule out intuition and other methods of sensing truth and reality. They are necessary even for the purposes of science. But always we must hold to our anchor of precise objective knowledge tested by reason and even more so by experiment and practice, and always we must beware of losing ourselves in a sea of speculation unconnected with the day-to-day problems of life and the needs of men and women. A living philosophy must answer the problems of today.

It may be that we of this modern age, who so pride ourselves on the achievements of our times, are prisoners of our age, just as the ancients and the men and women of medieval times were prisoners of their respective ages. We may delude ourselves, as others have done before us, that our way of looking at things is the only right way, leading to truth. We cannot escape from that prison or get rid entirely of that illusion, if illusion it is.

Yet I am convinced that the methods and approach of science have revolutionized human life more than anything else in the long course of history, and have opened doors and avenues of further and even more radical change, leading up to the very portals of what has long been considered the unknown. The technical achievements of science are obvious enough, its capacity to transform an economy of scarcity into one of abundance is evident, its invasion of many problems which have so far been the monopoly of philosophy is becoming more pronounced. Space-time and the Quantum Theory utterly changed the picture of the physical world. More recent researches into the nature of matter, the structure of the atom, the transmutation of the elements, and the transformation of electricity and light, either into the other, have carried human knowledge much further. Man no longer sees nature as something apart and distinct from himself. Human destiny appears to become a part of nature's rhythmic energy.

All this upheaval of thought, due to the advance of science, has led scientists into a new region, verging on the metaphysical. They draw different and often contradictory conclusions. Some see in it a new unity, the antithesis of chance. Others, like Bertrand Russell, say: 'Academic philosophers ever since the time of Parmenides have believed the world is unity. The most fundamental of my beliefs is that this is rubbish.' Or again: 'Man is the product of causes which had no prevision of the end they were achieving; his origin, his growth, his hopes and fears, his loves and beliefs are but the outcome of accidental collocations of atoms.' And yet the latest developments in physics have gone a long way to demonstrate a fundamental unity in nature. 'The belief that all things are made of a single substance is as old as thought itself ; but ours is the generation which, first of all in history, is able to perceive the unity of Nature not as a baseless dogma or a hopeless aspiration, but a principle of science based on

* Karl K. Darrow : *The Renaissance of Physics* (New York, 1936), p. 301.

proof as sharp and clear as anything which is known. *

Old as this belief is in Asia and Europe, it is interesting to compare some of the latest conclusions of science with the fundamental ideas underlying the *Advaita Vedantic* theory. These ideas were that the universe is made of one substance whose form is perpetually changing, and further that the sum-total of energies remains always the same. Also that 'the explanations of things are to be found within their own nature, and that no external beings or existences are required to explain what is going on in the universe, with its corollary of a self-evolving universe.

It does not very much matter to science what these vague speculations lead to, for meanwhile it forges ahead in a hundred directions, in its own precise experimental way of observation, widening the bounds of the charted region of knowledge, and changing human life in the process. It may be on the verge of discovering vital mysteries, and yet they may elude it. Still it will go on along its appointed path for there is no end to its journeying. Ignoring for the moment the *why* of philosophy, it will go on asking *how*, and as it finds this out it gives greater content and meaning to life, and perhaps takes us some way to answering the *why*.

Or, perhaps, we cannot cross that barrier, and the mysterious will continue to remain the mysterious, and life with all its changes will still remain a bundle of good and evil, a succession of conflicts, a curious combination of incompatible and mutually hostile urges.

Or again, perhaps, the very progress of science, unconnected with and isolated from moral discipline and ethical considerations, will lead to the concentration of power and the terrible instruments of destruction which it has made, in the hands of evil and selfish men, seeking the domination of others—and thus to the destruction of its own great achievements. Something of this kind we see happening now, and behind this war there lies this internal conflict of the spirit of man.

How amazing is this spirit of man ! In spite of innumerable failings, man, throughout the ages, has sacrificed his life and all he held dear for an ideal, for truth, for faith, for country and honour.

That ideal may change but that capacity for self-sacrifice continues, and, because of that, much may be forgiven to man, and it is impossible to lose hope for him. In the midst of disaster, he has not lost his dignity or his faith in the values he cherished. Plaything of nature's mighty forces, less than the speck of dust in this vast universe, he has hurled defiance at the elemental powers, and with his mind, cradle of revolution, sought to master them. Whatever gods there be, there is something godlike in man, as there is also something of the devil in him.

The future is dark, uncertain. But we can see part of the way leading to it and can tread it with firm steps, remembering that nothing that can happen is likely to overcome the spirit of man which has survived so many perils. Remembering also that life, for all its ills, has joy and beauty, and we can always wander, if we know how to, in the enchanted woods of nature.

> 'What else is Wisdom ? What of man's endeavour
> Or God's high grace, so lovely and so great ?
> To stand from fear set free, to breathe and wait;
> To hold a hand uplifted over Hate;
> And shall not Loveliness be loved for ever ?'

— Chorus from The Bacchae of Euripides—Gilbert Murray's translation.

The Discovery of India, 1946, pp. 9-17

CHAPTER 6
GROWTH AND DECAY

DURING the first thousand years of the Christian era, there are many ups and downs in India, many conflicts with invading elements and internal troubles. Yet it is a period of a vigorous national life, bubbling over with energy and spreading out in all directions. Culture develops into a rich civilization flowering out in philosophy, literature, drama, art, science and mathematics. India's economy expands, the Indian horizon widens and other countries come within its scope. Contacts grow with Iran, China, the Hellenic world, Central Asia and, above all, there is a powerful urge towards the eastern seas which leads to the establishment of Indian colonies and spread of Indian culture far beyond India's boundaries. During the middle period of this millennium, from early in the fourth to the sixth century, the Gupta Empire flourishes and becomes the patron and symbol of this widespread intellectual and artistic activity. That is called the Golden or Classical Age of India and in the writings of that period, which form the classics of Sanskrit literature, there is a quiet serenity, a confidence in themselves, and a glow of pride at being privileged to be alive in that high noon of civilization, and with this there is the urge to use their great intellectual and artistic powers to the utmost.

Yet even before that Golden Age had come to a close, signs of weakness and decay become visible. The White Huns come from the north-west in successive hordes and are repeatedly pushed back. But they come again and again and eat their way slowly into North India. For a half-century they even establish themselves as a ruling power all over the North. But then, with a great effort, the last of the great Guptas, joining up in a confederacy with Yashovarman, a ruler of Central India, drives out the Huns. This long-drawn-out conflict weakened India politically and militarily, and probably the settlement of large numbers of these Huns all over northern India gradually produced an inner change in the people. They were absorbed as all foreign elements had so far been absorbed, but they left their impress and weakened the old ideas of the Indo-Aryan races. Old accounts of the Huns are full of their excessive cruelty and barbarous behaviour which were so foreign to Indian standards of warfare and government.

In the seventh century there was a revival and renascence under Harsha, both political and cultural. Ujjayini (modern Ujjain), which had been the brilliant capital of the Guptas, again became a centre of art and culture and the seat of a powerful kingdom. But in the centuries that followed this too weakens and fades off. In the ninth century Mihira Bhoja of Gujarat consolidates a unified State in North and Central India with his capital at Kanauj. There is another literary revival of which the central figure is Rajashekhara. Again, at the beginning of the eleventh century, another Bhoja stands out as a powerful and attractive figure, and Ujjayini again becomes a great capital. This Bhoja was a remarkable man who distinguished himself in many fields. He was a grammarian and a lexicographer, and interested in medicine and astronomy. He was a builder and a patron of art and literature, and was himself a poet and a writer to whom many works are attributed. His name has become a part of popular fable and legend as a symbol of greatness, learning and generosity.

And yet for all these bright patches, an inner weakness seems to seize India which affects not only her political status but her creative activities. There is no date for this, for the process was a slow and creeping one and it affected North India earlier than the South. The South indeed becomes more important both politically and culturally. Perhaps this was due to the South having escaped the continuous strain of fighting waves of invaders; perhaps many of the writers and artists and master-builders migrated to the South to escape from the unsettled conditions in the North. The powerful kingdoms of the South, with their brilliant courts, must have attracted these people and given them opportunities for creative work which they lacked elsewhere.

But though the North did not dominate India, as it had often done in the past, and was split up into small States, life was still rich there and there were many centres of cultural and philosophic activity. Benares, as ever, was the heart of religious and philosophical thought, and every person who advanced a new theory, or a new interpretation of an old theory, had to come there to justify himself. Kashmir was for long a great Sanskrit centre of

Buddhist and Brahminical learning. The great universities flourished, Nalanda most famous of all, respected for its scholarship all over India. To have been to Nalanda was a hallmark of culture. It was not easy to enter that university, for admission was restricted to those who had already attained a certain standard. It specialized in post-graduate study and attracted students from China, Japan and Tibet and even, it is said, from Korea and Mongolia and Bokhara. Apart from religious and philosophical subjects (both Buddhist and Brahminical), secular and practical subjects were also taught. There was a school of art and a department for architecture; a medical school; an agricultural department; dairy farms and cattle. The intellectual life of the university is said to have been one of animated debates and discussions. The spread of Indian culture abroad was largely the work of scholars from Nalanda.

Then there was the Vikramshila University, near modern Bhagalpur in Bihar, and Vallabhi in Kathiawar. During the period of the Guptas, the Ujjayini University rose into prominence. In the south there was the Amravati University.

Yet, as the millennium approached its end, all this appears to be the afternoon of a civilization; the glow of the morning had long faded away, high noon was past. In the South there was still vitality and vigour and this lasted for some centuries more; in the Indian colonies abroad there was aggressive and full-blooded life right up to the middle of the next millennium. But the heart seems to petrify, its beats are slower, and gradually this petrifaction and decay spread to the limbs. There is no great figure in philosophy after Shankara in the eighth century, though there is a long succession of commentators and dialecticians. Even Shankara came from the South. The sense of curiosity and the spirit of mental adventure give place to a hard and formal logic and a sterile dialectic. Both Brahminism and Buddhism deteriorate and degraded forms of worship grow up, especially some varieties of *Tantric* worship and perversions of the *Yoga* system.

In literature, Bhavabhvuti (eighth century) is the last great figure. Many books continued to be written but their style becomes more and more involved and intricate; there is neither freshness of thought nor of expression. In mathematics Bhaskar II (twelfth century) is the last great name. In art, E. B. Havell takes us rather

beyond this period. He says that the form of expression was not
artistically perfected until about the seventh and eighth centuries,
when most of the great sculpture and painting in India was
produced. From the seventh or eighth to the fourteenth century,
according to him, was the great period of Indian art,
corresponding to the highest development of Gothic art in
Europe. He adds that it was in the sixteenth century that the
creative impulse of the old Indian art began markedly to diminish.
How far this judgement is correct I do not know, but I imagine that
even in the field of art it was South India that carried on the old
tradition for a longer period than the North.

The last of the major emigrations for colonial settlement took
place from South India in the ninth century, but the Cholas in the
South continued to be a great sea-power till the eleventh century
when they defeated and conquered Sri Vijaya.

We thus see that India was drying up and losing her creative
genius and vitality. The process was a slow one and lasted several
centuries, beginning in the North and finally reaching the South.
What were the causes of this political decline and cultural
stagnation ? Was this due to age alone, that seems to attack
civilizations as it does individuals, or to a kind of tidal wave with
its forward and backward motion ? Or were external causes and
invasions responsible for it ? Radhakrishnan says that Indian
philosophy lost its vigour with the loss of political freedom.
Sylvain Levi writes : 'La culture sanscrite a fini avec la liberté de
l'Inde; des langues nouvelles, des littératures nouvelles ont
envahi la territoire aryen et l'en ont chassée; elle s'est réfugié
dans les collèges et y a pris un air pédantèsque.'

All this is true for the loss of political freedom leads inevitably to
cultural decay. But why should political freedom be lost unless
some kind of decay has preceded it ? A small country might easily
be overwhelmed by superior power, but a huge, well-developed
and highly civilized country like India, cannot succumb to external
attack unless there is internal decay, or the invader possesses a
higher technique of warfare. That internal decay is clearly evident
in India at the close of these thousand years.

There are repeatedly periods of decay and disruption in the life
of every civilization and there had been such periods in Indian
history previously. But India had survived them and rejuvenated

herself afresh, sometimes retiring into her shell for a while and emerging again with fresh vigour. There always remained a dynamic core which could renew itself with fresh contacts and develop again, something different from the past and yet intimately connected with it. Had that capacity for adaptation, that flexibility of mind which had saved India so often in the past left her now ? Had her fixed beliefs and the growing rigidity of her social structure made her mind also rigid ? For if life ceases to grow and evolve, the evolution of thought also ceases. India had all along been a curious combination of conservatism in practice and explosive thought. Inevitably that thought affected the practice, though it did so in its own way without irreverence for the past. Mais si leur yeux suivaient les mots anciens, leur intelligence y voyait des ideés nouvelles. L'Inde s'est transformée à son insu.' But when thought lost its explosiveness and creative power and became a tame attendant on an outworn and meaningless practice, mumbling old phrases and fearful of everything new, then life became stagnant and tied and constrained in a prison of its own making.

We have many examples of the collapse of a civilization and perhaps the most notable of these is that of the European classical civilization which ended with the fall of Rome. Long before Rome fell to the invaders from the north, it had been on the verge of collapse from its own internal weaknesses. Its economy, once expanding, had shrunk and brought all manner of difficulties in its train. Urban industries decayed, flourishing cities grew progressively smaller and impoverished, and even fertility rapidly declined. The Emperors tried many expedients to overcome their ever-increasing difficulties. There was compulsory State regulation of merchants, craftsmen and workers, who were tied down to particular employments. Many kinds of employees were even forbidden to marry outside their own group of workers. Thus some occupations were practically converted into castes. The peasantry became serfs. But all these superficial attempts to check the decline failed and even worsened conditions; and the Roman Empire collapsed.

There was and has been no such dramatic collapse of Indian civilization and it has shown an amazing staying power despite all that has happened. But a progressive decline is visible. It is difficult to specify in any detail what the social conditions in India were at the end of the first millennium after Christ. But it may be said with some assurance that the expanding economy of India had ended and there was a strong tendency to shrink. Probably this was the inevitable result of the growing rigidity and exclusiveness of the Indian social structure as represented chiefly by the caste system. Where Indians had gone abroad, as in South-East Asia, they were not so rigid in mind or customs or in their economy, and they had opportunities for growth and expansion. For another four or five hundred years they flourished in these colonies and displayed energy and creative vigour. But in India herself the spirit of exclusiveness sapped the creative faculty and developed a narrow, small-group, and parochial outlook. Life became all cut up into set frames where each man's job was fixed and permanent and he had little concern with others. It was the *Kshatriya's* business to fight in defence of the country and others were not interested or were not even allowed to do so. The Brahmin and the *Kshatriya* looked down on trade and commerce. Education and opportunities of growth were withheld from the lower castes, who were taught to be submissive to those higher up in the scale. In spite of a well-developed urban economy and industries, the structure of the State was in many ways feudal. Probably even in the technique of warfare India had fallen behind. No marked progress was possible under these conditions without changing that structure and releasing fresh sources of talent and energy. The caste system was a barrier to such a change. For all its virtues and the stability it had given to Indian society, it carried within it the seeds of destruction.

The Indian social structure (and I shall consider this more fully later) had given amazing stability to Indian civilization. It had given strength and cohesion to the group, but this came in the way of expansion and a larger cohesion. It developed crafts and skill and trade and commerce, but always within each group separately. Thus particular types of activity became hereditary and there was a tendency to avoid new types of work and activity and to confine oneself to the old groove, to restrict initiative and the spirit of innovation. It gave a measure of freedom within a certain limited sphere, but at the expense of the growth of a larger freedom and at the heavy price of keeping large numbers of people permanently at the bottom of the social ladder, deprived of the opportunities of growth. So long as that structure afforded avenues for growth and expansion, it was progressive; when it reached the limits of expansion open to it, it became stationary, unprogressive and, later, inevitably regressive.

Because of this there was decline all along the line — intellectual, philosophical, political, in technique and methods of warfare, in knowledge of and contacts with the outside world, and there was a growth of local sentiments and feudal and small-group feeling at the expense of the larger conception of India as a whole, and in a shrinking economy. Yet, as later ages were to show, there was yet vitality in the old structure and an amazing tenacity, as well as some flexibility and capacity for adaptation. Because of this it managed to survive and to profit by new contacts and waves of thought, and even progress in some ways. But that progress was always tied down to and hampered by far too many relics of the past.

The Discovery of India, 1946, pp. 187-89

CHAPTER 7

DEVELOPMENT OF
A COMMON CULTURE

AKBAR had built so well that the edifice he had erected lasted for another hundred years in spite of inadequate successors. After almost every Moghul reign there were wars between the princes for the throne, thus weakening the central power. But the court continued to be brilliant and the fame of the Grand Moghul spread all over Asia and Europe. Beautiful buildings combining the old Indian ideals in architecture with a new simplicity and a nobility of line grew up in Agra and Delhi. This Indo-Moghul art was in marked contrast with the decadent, over-elaborate and heavily ornamented temples and other buildings of the North and South. Inspired architects and builders put up with loving hands the Taj Mahal at Agra.

The last of the so-called 'Grand Moghuls', Aurungzeb, tried to put back the clock and in this attempt stopped it and broke it up The Moghul rulers were strong so long as they put themselves in line with the genius of the nation and tried to work for a common nationality and a synthesis of the various elements in the country. When Aurungzeb began to oppose this movement and suppress it and to function more as a Moslem than an Indian ruler, the Moghul Empire began to break up. The work of Akbar, and to some extent his successors, was undone and the various forces that had been kept in check by Akbar's policy broke loose and challenged that empire. New movements arose, narrow in outlook but representing a resurgent nationalism, and though they were not strong enough to build permanently, and circumstances were against them, they were capable of destroying the empire of the Moghuls.

The impact of the invaders from the north-west and of Islam on India had been considerable. It had pointed out and shown up the abuses that had crept into Hindu society — the petrifaction of caste, untouchability, exclusiveness carried to fantastic lengths. The idea of the brotherhood of Islam and of the theoretical equality of its adherents made a powerful appeal, especially to those in the

Hindu fold who were denied any semblance of equal treatment. From this ideological impact grew up various movements aiming at a religious synthesis. Many conversions also took place but the great majority of these were from the lower castes, especially in Bengal. Some individuals belonging to the higher castes also adopted the new faith, either because of a real change of belief or, more often, for political and economic reasons. There were obvious advantages in accepting the religion of the ruling power.

In spite of these widespread conversions, Hinduism, in all its varieties, continued as the dominant faith of the land, solid, exclusive, self-sufficient and sure of itself. The upper castes had no doubt about their own superiority in the realm of ideas and thought and considered Islam as a rather crude approach to the problems of philosophy and metaphysics. Even the monotheism of Islam they found in their own religion, together with monism which was the basis of much of their philosophy. Each person could take his choice of these or of more popular and simpler forms of worship. He could be a *Vaishnavite* and believe in a personal God and pour out his faith to him. Or, more philosophically inclined, he could wander in the tenuous realms of metaphysics and high philosophy. Though all their social structure was based on the group, in matters of religion they were highly individualistic, not believing in proselytization themselves and caring little if some people were converted to another faith. What was objected to was an interference with their own social structure and ways of living. If another group wanted to function in it own way, it was at liberty to do so. It is worth noting that, as a rule, conversions to Islam were group conversions, so powerful was the influence of the group. Among the upper castes individuals might change their religion, but lower down the scale a particular caste in a locality, or almost an entire village would be converted. Thus their group life as well as their functions continued as before with only minor variations as regards worship, etc. Because of this we find today particular occupations and crafts almost entirely monopolized by Moslems. Thus the class of weavers is predominantly, and in large areas entirely, Moslem. So also used to be shoe-merchants and butchers. Tailors are almost always Moslems. Various kinds of artisans and craftsmen are Moslems. Owing to the breaking up of the group system, many individuals have taken to other occupations and this has somewhat obliterated the line dividing the various occupational groups. The destruction of crafts and village industries, originally deliberately undertaken under early British rule and later resulting from the development of a new colonial economy, led to vast numbers of these artisans and craftsmen, more especially the weavers, being deprived of their occupations and livelihood. Those who survived this catastrophe drifted to the land and became landless labourers or shared a tiny patch of land with their relatives.

Conversions to Islam in those days, whether individual or group, probably aroused no particular opposition, except when force or some kind of compulsion was used. Friends and relatives or neighbours might disapprove, but the Hindu community as such apparently attached little importance to this. In contrast with this indifferent attitude, conversions today attract widespread attention and are resented, whether they are to Islam or Christianity. This is largely due to political factors and especially to the introduction of separate religious electorates. Each convert is supposed to be a gain to the communal group leading ultimately to greater representation and more political power. Attempts are even made to manipulate the census to this end. Apart from political reasons, there has also been a growth in Hinduism of a tendency to proselytize and convert non-Hindus to Hinduism. This is one of the direct effects of Islam on Hinduism, though in practice it brings it into conflict with Islam in India. Orthodox Hindus still do not approve of it.

In Kashmir a long-continued process of conversion to Islam had resulted in 95 per cent of the population becoming Moslems, though they retained many of their old Hindu customs. In the middle nineteenth century the Hindu ruler of the State found that very large numbers of these people were anxious or willing to return *en bloc* to Hinduism. He sent a deputation to the pundits of Benares inquiring if this could be done. The pundits refused to countenance any such change of faith and there the matter ended.

The Moslems who came to India from outside brought no new technique or political and economic structure. In spite of a religious belief in the brotherhood of Islam, they were class bound and feudal in outlook. In technique and in the methods of production and industrial organization, they were inferior to what prevailed then in India. Thus their influence on the economic life of India and the social structure was very little. This life continued as of old and all the people, Hindu or Moslem or others, fitted into it.

The position of women deteriorated. Even the ancient laws had been unfair to them in regard to inheritance and their position in the household–though even so they were fairer than nineteenth century English law. Those laws of inheritance derived from the Hindu joint family system and sought to protect joint property from transfer to another family. A woman by marriage changed her family. In an economic sense she was looked upon as a dependent of her father or husband or son, but she could and did hold property in her own right. In many ways she was honoured and respected and had a fair measure of freedom, taking part in social and cultural activities. Indian history is full of the names of famous women, including thinkers and philosophers, rulers and warriors. This freedom grew progressively less. Islam had a fairer law of inheritance but this did not affect Hindu women. What did affect many of them to their great disadvantage, as it affected Moslem women to a much greater degree, was the intensification of the custom of seclusion of women. This spread among the upper classes all over the North and in Bengal, but the South and West of India escaped this degrading custom. Even in the North, only the upper classes indulged in it and the masses were happily free from it. Women now had less chances of education and their activities were largely confined to the household.* Lacking most other ways of distinguishing themselves, living a confined and restricted life, they were told that their supreme virtue lay in chastity and the supreme sin in a loss of it. Such was the man-made doctrine, but man did not apply it to himself. Tulsidas in his deservedly famous poem, the Hindi *Ramayana*, written during Jehangir's time, painted a picture of woman which is grossly unfair and prejudiced.

Partly because the great majority of Moslems in India were converts from Hinduism, partly because of long contact, Hindus

---

* And yet many instances of notable women, scholars as well as rulers, occur even during this period and later. In the eighteenth century Lakshmi Devi wrote a great legal commentary on the Mitakshara, a famous law book of the medieval period.

and Moslems in India developed numerous common traits, habits, ways of living and artistic tastes, especially in northern India-in music, painting, architecture, food, clothes, and common traditions. They lived together peacefully as one people, joined each other's festivals and celebrations, spoke the same language, lived in more or less the same way, and faced identical economic problems. The nobility and the landed gentry and their numerous hangers-on took their cue from the court. (These people were not landlords or owners of the land. They did not take rent but were allowed to collect and retain the State revenue for a particular area. These grants were usually for life.) They developed a highly intricate and sophisticated common culture. They wore the same kind of clothes, ate the same type of food, had common artistic pursuits, military pastimes, hunting, chivalry and games. Polo was a favourite game, and elephant fights were popular.

All this intercourse and common living took place in spite of the caste system which prevented fusion. There were no intermarriages except in rare instances and even then it was not fusion but usually the transfer of a Hindu woman to the Moslem fold. Nor was there inter-dining but this was not so strict. The seclusion of women prevented the development of social life. This applied even more to Moslems *inter se,* for purdah among them was stricter. Though Hindu and Moslem men met each other frequently, such opportunities were lacking to the women of both groups. These women of the nobility and upper classes were thus far more cut off from each other and developed much more marked separate ideological groups, each largely ignorant of the other.

Among the common people in the villages, and that means the vast majority of the population, life had a much more corporate and joint basis. Within the limited circle of the village there was an intimate •relationship between the Hindus and Moslems. Caste did not come in the way and the Hindus looked upon the Moslems as belonging to another caste. Most of the Moslems were converts who were still full of their old traditions. They were well acquainted with the Hindu background, mythology and epic stories. They did the same kind of work, lived similar lives, wore the same kind of clothes, spoke the same language. They joined each other's festivals and some semi-religious festivals were common to both. They had common folk songs. Mostly these people were peasants and artisans and craftsmen.

The third large group, in between the nobility and the peasantry and artisans, was the merchant and trader class. This was predominantly Hindu and though it had no political power, the economic structure was largely under its control. This class had fewer intimate contacts with the Moslems than any other class, above it or below. The Moslems who had come from outside India were feudal in outlook and did not take kindly to trade. The Islamic prohibition against the taking of interest also came in the way of trade. They considered themselves the ruling class, the nobility, and functioned as State officials, holders of grants of land or as officers in the army. There were also many scholars attached to the court or in charge of theological and other academies.

During the Moghul period large numbers of Hindus wrote books in Persian which was the official court language. Some of these books have become classics of their kind. At the same time Moslem scholars translated Sanskrit books into Persian and wrote in Hindi. Two of the best known Hindi poets are Malik Mohammad Jaisi, who wrote the *Padmavat*, and Abdul Rahim Khankhana, one of the premier nobles of Akbar's court and son of his guardian. Khankhana was a scholar in Arabic, Persian and Sanskrit and his Hindi poetry is of a high quality. For some time he was the commander-in-chief of the imperial army, and yet he has written in praise and admiration of Rana Pratap of Mewar, who was continually fighting Akbar and never submitted to him. Khankhana admires and commends the patriotism and high sense of honour and chivalry of his enemy on the battlefield.

It was this chivalrous and friendly approach on which Akbar based his policy and which many of his counsellors and ministers learned from him. He was particularly attached to the Rajputs for he admired in them qualities which he himself possessed — reckless courage, a sense of honour and chivalry, and an adherence to the pledged word. He won over the Rajputs, but the Rajputs, for all their admirable qualities, represented a medieval type of society which was already becoming out of date as new forces were arising. Akbar was not conscious of these new forces for he himself was a prisoner of his own social inheritance.

Akbar's success is astonishing for he created a sense of oneness among the diverse elements of North and Central India. There was the barrier of a ruling class, mainly of foreign origin, and there were the barriers of religion and caste, a proselytizing religion opposed to a static but highly resistant system. These barriers did not disappear but in spite of them that feeling of oneness grew. It was not merely an attachment to his person; it was an attachment to the structure he had built. His son and grandson, Jehangir and Shah Jehan, accepted that structure and functioned within its framework. They were men of no outstanding ability but their reigns were successful because they continued on the lines so firmly laid down by Akbar. The next comer, Aurungzeb, much abler but of a different mould, swerved and left that beaten track, undoing Akbar's work. Yet not entirely, for it is extraordinary how, in spite of him and his feeble and pitiful successors, that feeling of reverence for that structure continued. That feeling was largely confined to the North and centre; it did not extend to the South or West. And it was from western India, therefore, that the challenge to it came.

The Discovery of India, 1946, pp. 224-29

CHAPTER 8
AND THEN GANDHI CAME

WORLD WAR I came. Politics were at a low ebb, chiefly because of the split in the Congress between the two sections, the so-called Extremists and the Moderates, and because of war-time restrictions and regulations. Yet one tendency was marked : the rising middle-class among the Moslems was growing more nationally-minded and was pushing the Moslem League towards the Congress. They even joined hands.

Industry developed during the War and produced enormous dividends—100% to 200% from the jute mills of Bengal and the cotton mills of Bombay, Ahmedabad and elsewhere. Some of these dividends flowed to the owners of foreign capital in Dundee and London, some went to swell the riches of Indian millionaires. And yet the workers who had created these dividends lived at an incredibly low level of existence—in 'filthy, disease-ridden hovels' with no window or chimney, no light or water-supply, no sanitary arrangements. This near that so-called city of palaces, Calcutta, dominated by British capital. In Bombay, where Indian capital was more in evidence, an inquiry commission found in one room, 15 feet by 12, six families, in all thirty adults and children, living together. Three of these women were expecting a confinement soon, and each family had a separate oven in that one room. These are special cases, but they are not very exceptional. They describe conditions in the twenties and thirties of this century when some improvements had already been made. What these conditions were like previous to these improvements staggers the imagination.*

I remember visiting some of these slums and hovels of industrial workers, gasping for breath there, and coming out dazed and full of horror and anger. I remember also going down a coal mine in Jharia and seeing the conditions in which our womenfolk worked there. I can never forget that picture or the shock that came to me

---

* These quotations and facts are taken from B.Shiva Rao's 'The Industrial Worker in India' (Allen and Unwin, London, 1939) which deals with labour-problems and workers' conditions in India.

that human beings should labour thus. Women were
subsequently prohibited from working underground. But now
they have been sent back there because, we are told, war needs
require additional labour. And yet millions of men are starving
and unemployed; there is no lack of men. But the wages are so low
and the conditions of work so bad that they do not attract.

A delegation sent by the British Trade Union Congress visited
India in 1928. In their report they said that 'In Assam tea the sweat,
hunger, and despair of a million Indians enter year by year'. The
Director of Public Health in Bengal in his Report for 1927-28 said
that the peasantry of that province were 'taking to a dietary on
which even rats could not live for more than five weeks'.

World War I ended at last and the peace, instead of bringing us
relief and progress, brought us repressive legislation and Martial
Law in the Punjab. A bitter sense of humiliation and a passionate
anger filled our people. All the unending talk of constitutional
reform and indianization of the services was a mockery and an
insult when the manhood of our country was being crushed and
the inexorable and continuous process of exploitation was
deepening our poverty and sapping our vitality. We had become
a derelict nation.

Yet what could we do, how change this vicious process ? We
seemed to be helpless in the grip of some all-powerful monster;
our limbs were paralyzed, our minds deadened. The peasantry
were servile and fear-ridden, the industrial workers were no
better. The middle classes, the intelligentsia, who might have been
beacon-lights in the enveloping darkness, were themselves
submerged in this all-pervading gloom. In some ways their
condition was even more pitiful than that of the peasantry. Large
numbers of the *déclassé* intellectuals, cut off from the land and
incapable of any kind of manual or technical work, joined the
swelling army of the unemployed and helpless, hopeless, sank
ever deeper into the morass. A few successful lawyers or doctors
or engineers or clerks made little difference to the mass. The
peasant starved, yet centuries of an unequal struggle against his
environment had taught him to endure, and even in poverty and
starvation he had a certain calm dignity, a feeling of submission to
an all-powerful fate. Not so the middle classes, more especially the
new petty bourgeoisie, who had no such background.

Incompletely developed and frustrated, they did not know where to look, for neither the old nor the new offered them any hope. There was no adjustment to social purpose, no satisfaction of doing something worthwhile, even though suffering came in its train. Custom-ridden, they were born old, yet they were without the old culture. Modern thought attracted them but they lacked its inner content, the modern social and scientific consciousness. Some tried to cling tenaciously to the dead forms of the past, seeking relief from present misery in them. But there could be no relief there for, as Tagore has said, we must not nourish in our being what is dead, for the dead is death-dealing. Others made themselves pale and ineffectual copies of the West. So, like derelicts, frantically seeking some foothold of security for body and mind and finding none, they floated aimlessly in the murky waters of Indian life.

What could we do ? How could we pull India out of this quagmire of poverty and defeatism which sucked her in ? Not for a few years of excitement and agony and suspense, but for long generations our people had offered their 'blood and toil, tears and sweat'. And this process had eaten its way deep into the body and soul of India, poisoning every aspect of our corporate life, like that fell disease which consumes the tissues of the lungs and kills slowly but inevitably. Sometimes we thought that some swifter and more obvious process, resembling cholera or the bubonic plague, would have been better. But that was a passing thought for adventurism leads nowhere, and the quack treatment of deep-seated diseases does not yield results.

And then Gandhi came. He was like a powerful current of fresh air that made us stretch ourselves and take deep breaths, like a beam of light that pierced the darkness and removed the scales from our eyes, like a whirlwind that upset many things but most of all the working of people's minds. He did not descend from the top: he seemed to emerge from the millions of India, speaking their language and incessantly drawing attention to them and their appalling condition. Get off the backs of these peasants and workers, he told us, all you who live by their exploitation: get rid of the system that produces this poverty and misery. Political freedom took new shape then and acquired a new content. Much that he said we only partially accepted or sometimes did not accept at all. But all this was secondary. The essence of his teaching was fearlessness and truth and action allied to these, always keeping the welfare of the masses in view. The greatest gift for an individual or a nation, so we had been told in our ancient books, was *abhaya*, fearlessness, not merely bodily courage but the absence of fear from the mind. Janaka and Yajnavalka had said, at the dawn of our history, that it was the function of the leaders of a people to make them fearless. But the dominant impulse in India under British rule was that of fear, pervasive, oppressing, strangling fear; fear of the army, the police, the widespread secret service; fear of the official class; fear of laws meant to suppress and of prison; fear of the landlord's agent; fear of the money-lender; fear of unemployment and starvation, which were always on the threshold. It was against this all-pervading fear that Gandhi's quiet and determined voice was raised: Be not afraid. Was it so simple as all that? Not quite. And yet fear builds its phantoms which are more fearsome than reality itself, and reality when calmly analyzed and its consequences willingly accepted, loses much of its terror.

So, suddenly as it were, that black pall of fear was lifted from the people's shoulders, not wholly of course, but to an amazing degree. As fear is close companion to falsehood, so truth follows fearlessness. The Indian people did not become much more truthful than they were, nor did they change their essential nature overnight; nevertheless a sea-change was visible as the need for falsehood and furtive behaviour lessened. It was a psychological change, almost as if some expert in psycho-analytical method had probed deep into the patient's past, found out the origins of his complexes, exposed them to his view, and thus rid him of that burden.

There was that psychological reaction also, a feeling of shame at our long submission to an alien rule that had degraded and humiliated us, and a desire to submit no longer whatever the consequences might be.

We did not grow much more truthful perhaps than we had been previously, but Gandhi was always there as a symbol of uncompromising truth to pull us up and shame us into truth. What is truth? I do not know for certain, and perhaps our truths are relative and absolute truth is beyond us. Different persons may and do take different views of truth and each individual is powerfully influenced by his own background, training and impulses. So also Gandhi. But truth is at least for an individual what he himself feels and knows to be true. According to that definition I do not know of any person who holds to the truth as Gandhi does. That is a dangerous quality in a politician for he speaks out his mind and even lets the public see its changing phases.

Gandhi influenced millions of people in India in varying degrees; some changed the whole texture of their lives, others were only partly affected, or the effect wore off, and yet not quite, for some part of it could not be wholly shaken off. Different people reacted differently and each will give his own answer to this question. Some might well say almost in the words of Alcibiades: 'Besides, when we listen to any one else talking, however eloquent he is, we don't really care a damn what he says; but when we listen to you, or to some one else repeating what you've said, even if he puts it ever so badly, and never mind whether the person who is listening is man, woman, or child, we're absolutely staggered and bewitched. And speaking for myself, gentlemen, if I wasn't afraid you'd tell me I was completely bottled, I'd swear on oath what an extraordinary effect his words have had on me—and still do, if it comes to that. For the moment I hear him speak I am smitten by a kind of sacred rage, worse than any Corybant, and my heart jumps into my mouth and the tears start into my eyes—Oh, and not only me, but lots of other men.

'Yes, I have heard Pericles and all the other great orators, and very eloquent I thought they were; but they never affected me like that; they never turned my whole soul upside down and left me feeling as if I were the lowest of the low; but this latter day Maryas here, has often left me in such a state of mind that I've felt I simply couldn't go on living the way I did...

'And there is one thing I've never felt with anybody else—not the kind of thing you would expect to find in me, either—and that is a sense of shame. Socrates is the only man in the world that can make me feel ashamed. Because there's no getting away from it, I know I ought to do the things he tells me to; and yet the moment I'm out of his sight I don't care what I do to keep in with the mob. So I dash off like a runaway slave, and keep out of his way as long as I can: and then next time I meet him I remember all that I had to admit the time before, and naturally I feel ashamed...

'Only I've been bitten by something much more poisonous than a snake; in fact, mine is the most painful kind of bite there is. I've been bitten in the heart, or the mind, or whatever you like to call it... *

The Discovery of India, 1946, pp. 309-13

* From 'The Five Dialogues of Plato', Everyman's Library.

CHAPTER 9
TRYST WITH DESTINY

LONG years ago we made a tryst with destiny, and now the time comes when we shall redeem our pledge, not wholly or in full measure, but very substantially. At the stroke of the midnight hour, when the world sleeps, India will awake to life and freedom. A moment comes, which comes but rarely in history, when we step out from the old to the new, when an age ends, and when the soul of a nation, long suppressed, finds utterance. It is fitting that at this solemn moment we take the pledge of dedication to the service of India and her people and to the still larger cause of humanity.

At the dawn of history India started on her unending quest, and trackless centuries are filled with her striving and the grandeur of her success and her failures. Through good and ill fortune alike she has never lost sight of that quest or forgotten the ideals which gave her strength. We end today a period of ill fortune and India discovers herself again. The achievement we celebrate today is but a step, an opening of opportunity, to the greater triumphs and achievements that await us. Are we brave enough and wise enough to grasp this opportunity and accept the challenge of the future?

Freedom and power bring responsibility. The responsibility rests upon this Assembly, a sovereign body representing the sovereign people of India. Before the birth of freedom we have endured all the pains of labour and our hearts are heavy with the memory of this sorrow. Some of those pains continue even now. Nevertheless, the past is over and it is the future that beckons to us now.

That future is not one of ease or resting but of incessant striving so that we may fulfil the pledges we have so often taken and the one we shall take today. The service of India means the service of the millions who suffer. It means the ending of poverty and ignorance and disease and inequality of opportunity. The ambition of the greatest man of our generation has been to wipe every tear from every eye. That may be beyond us, but as long as there are tears and suffering, so long our work will not be over.

And so we have to labour and to work, and work hard, to give reality to our dreams. Those dreams are for India, but they are also for the world, for all the nations and peoples are too closely knit together today for any one of them to imagine that it can live apart. Peace has been said to be indivisible; so is freedom, so is prosperity now, and so also is disaster in this One World that can no longer be split into isolated fragments.

To the people of India, whose representatives we are, we make an appeal to join us with faith and confidence in this great adventure. This is no time for petty and destructive criticism, no time for ill will or blaming others. We have to build the noble mansion of free India where all her children may dwell.

Selected Works of Jawaharlal Nehru, Second Series, 1985, III, pp. 135-36. Speech in the Constituent Assembly at midnight of 14-15 August 1947 on the eve of independence. First recorded in *Constituent Assembly Debates, Official Report*, V, 1947, pp. 4-5.

·

THE appointed day has come—the day appointed by destiny—and India stands forth again after long slumber and struggle, awake, vital, free and independent. The past clings on to us still in some measure and we have to do much before we redeem the pledges we have so often taken. Yet the turning point is past, and history begins anew for us, the history which we shall live and act and others will write about.

It is a fateful moment for us in India, for all Asia and for the world. A new star rises, the star of freedom in the East, a new hope comes into being, a vision long cherished materializes. May the star never set and that hope never be betrayed!

We rejoice in that freedom, even though clouds surround us, and many of our people are sorrow-stricken and difficult problems encompass us. But freedom brings responsibilities and burdens and we have to face them in the spirit of a free and disciplined people.

On this day our first thoughts go to the architect of this freedom, the Father of our Nation, who, embodying the old spirit of India, held aloft the torch of freedom and lighted up the darkness that surrounded us. We have often been unworthy followers of his and have strayed from his message, but not only we but succeeding generations will remember this message and bear the imprint in their hearts of this great son of India, magnificent in his faith and strength and courage and humility. We shall never allow that torch of freedom to be blown out, however high the wind or stormy the tempest.

Our next thoughts must be of the unknown volunteers and soldiers of freedom who, without praise or reward, have served India even unto death.

We think also of our brothers and sisters who have been cut off from us by political boundaries and who unhappily cannot share at present in the freedom that has come. They are of us and will remain of us whatever may happen, and we shall be sharers in their good and ill fortune alike.

The future beckons to us. Whither do we go and what shall be our endeavour? To bring freedom and opportunity to the common man, to the peasants and workers of India; to fight and end poverty and ignorance and disease; to build up a prosperous, democratic and progressive nation, and to create social, economic and political institutions which will ensure justice and fullness of life to every man and woman.

We have hard work ahead. There is no resting for any one of us till we redeem our pledge in full, till we make all the people of India what destiny intended them to be. We are citizens of a great country, on the verge of bold advance, and we have to live up to that high standard. All of us, to whatever religion we may belong, are equally the children of India with equal rights, privileges and obligations. We cannot encourage communalism or narrow-mindedness, for no nation can be great whose people are narrow in thought or in action.

To the nations and peoples of the world we send greetings and pledge ourselves to co-operate with them in furthering peace, freedom and democracy.

And to India, our much-loved motherland, the ancient, the eternal and the ever-new, we pay our reverent homage and we bind ourselves afresh to her service. Jai Hind.

Selected Works of Jawaharlal Nehru, Second Series, 1985, III, pp. 49-50. Message to the nation on Independence Day printed in the newspapers (*Hindusthan Standard The Statesman*) on 15 August 1947.

CHAPTER 10

THE CULTIVATION OF
A SCIENTIFIC OUTLOOK

CULTURE is one of those which might mean anything, including culture in everything, in history, in society and in every form of human activity.

Certain people in this country, for instance, condemn education in India as a manifestation of British imperialism. I suppose there is nobody in India who is not aware of the fact that the present system of education is bad, and that the basis on which it stands is doubly bad. Attempts are, however, being continually made to change and improve it.

The Wardha scheme of education seems to me a remarkable attempt at improvement of education on modern lines. I am of the opinion that any system of education that might be introduced in this country should integrate the activities of both the mind and the body of the students.

What exactly do you mean by culture? Individual culture, social and national developments and everything akin to them. Development also takes two forms generally. There is the development of individuals which is highly important, and as individuals develop they form social groups. Naturally the more well-developed the individuals, the higher the social groups which we shall have. On the other hand, when we develop a social group, it helps the development of individuals, because one reacts upon the other. So we have to see that both developments take place simultaneously.

Ordinarily, the religious approach in the past has been the way of individual development. It tries to improve the individual hoping that the improvement of the individual will affect the social group. That has been so in every country whatever religion it may have had or whatever method may have been devised for approaching the problem.

Nevertheless, the modern method lays stress on improving the environment so that a person living in a particular environment may grow to his fullest capacity. Both these methods have not been, however, contemporary. Perhaps the stress laid on the improvement of a particular environment is more important today because if the environment is bad you cannot make much progress. We have to think again in terms of social culture and what kind of environment it develops. What is the good, for instance, of your trying to cultivate unselfishness and noble qualities when the social structure that surrounds you is based on selfishness and produces bad influences on life?

Look at the world today, the international world. It is quite astoundingly immoral and bad. How can you expect influences to be highly moral when continuous pressure of immorality is put on environments, with the result that there has inevitably occurred an all-round deterioration. The deterioration has taken place on the international level, the national level and the individual level.

Today there is a great feeling of paralysis of mind among a large number of thinking individuals in Europe, in America and all over the world. It is so because they feel that the forces of evil are stronger than their combined strength. The forces of evil are indicated by fascism and reaction, and this environment forces them to be far from good.

How to find a way out of this situation? It is not enough for you to imagine that the problem is so simple that by a few slogans you will be able to solve it. Every form of government or state, whether it is fascist, imperialist or communist, indulges inevitably in creating an environment which helps its maintenance. It inevitably tries to spread its influence on the minds of its citizens through educational process.

You have, therefore, ultimately to decide what form of state or society you are going to have. Saying that you dislike imperialism is to make a negative statement. We have to be positive as to what type of 'ism' we want. It depends on certain fundamental axioms of thought and freedom of various kinds of activities. Because various complex situations influence the society as well as the individual, we cannot possibly help develop the conditions we desire.

We must, therefore, have freedom of thought. We must have a democratic process working as far as it can. But, at the same time, we must not forget that the freedom of thought leads to some difficulties. Ordinarily, it does not lead to difficulties because people who avail of the freedom of thought and action are sufficiently disciplined. They are advanced in their thinking and are responsible in outlook.

Today in many countries of the world the democratic process seems to work slow. It does not bring in results quickly when quick results are necessary. We, therefore, find that in this century democracy has not functioned well even in those countries where it has been in existence for many years. When confronted with these difficulties we try to find an answer by resorting to pet phrases which do not really help. They only divert our attention to other channels of thought.

Today mankind is passing through unprecedented changes, and a period of transition. We must remember that we are going through the most extraordinary period in history. It has been an astoundingly revolutionary period of changes. From my knowledge of history, I doubt if there has hitherto been any time which was fraught with such revolutionary changes as the period which began in 1914 with the commencement of the Great War and which continues till today.

It is not a question of one year or two. This crisis of change is bound to remain with us for a long time to come.

You hear nowadays a great deal about planning, specially in industrial and economic life; but what is more important is the planning of various activities of life that the nation undertakes so that each activity fits in well with the other. Yet, the approach to the problems must be our own.

In India today there is a conflict going on between two kinds of forces and problems. It is more or less a psychological conflict. There are obviously other conflicts such as political, economic and others. But there is also a psychological conflict, a conflict of minds. Many forces are pulling us in different directions. Many forces of the past have strengthened us. Many others have proved a burden also.

Now look at the various complex forces that have resulted in developing a more or less composite culture in this country. Every culture is equally a composite culture because no culture is purely a national culture in the sense that it has had no influence from other quarters. Of course, there is such a phenomenon as national culture which has a certain influence on the nation, but, generally speaking, even this culture has had a great deal of influence from other quarters, although India is one of those countries which has had an essentially composite culture for thousands of years. Our country has possessed a great capacity for absorbing foreign cultures that invaded this country.

Ultimately, India had to face what we call a new culture from the West which had as its basis science and modern industry which upset for the time being the whole fabric. During the last one hundred years or so, there has been a conflict in India between various types of cultures. There has been a conflict between the Western culture and our own culture. I do not mean to say that there is essentially a conflict between the two in public ; but still there is an inherent conflict. If the culture of the West had not come to us in the guise of political conquerors there would not have been any conflict.

Just as in other cases we would have taken it much more readily, we must distinguish it from this political conquest because science as such has nothing to do with political conquest. It is something which represents the spirit of the age. There cannot be any doubt that we cannot progress nationally or individually unless we profit by the lessons of science.

There is, however, a problem before us when we think of science. We have to think presumably not of science as applied in the fields of industry or politics but science in its wider connotation. What is science ? It is a certain way of approaching problems, a certain way of seeking the truth. It is a certain empirical way whereby we get prepared to reject anything if we cannot establish or prove it.

Of course, some of the most established rules of science are often being upset. Newton's theory of gravitation has undergone a change by Einstein's theory.

What I wish to emphasize is that science means an approach to all of life's problems. It is to be applied to the problems relating to our family, religion and everything else. You cannot apply science in your industries keeping other departments of your life free from it. The whole scheme is unscientific. Therefore, if we want to consider various problems that face us as an individual and as a social group, the right way to consider these problems is to adopt the method of science. If we examine our social and economic systems, we will find that these have developed in a most irrational manner. If on one side there is an abundance of production, we find that on the other side there is terrible misery and want.

The League of Nations proclaims peace and cooperation but the very members of the League are preparing for war and indulging in wars of aggression. They are the people destroying foodstuffs so that the prices of those foodstuffs might be kept up for profit *. If we want to solve all these problems, we have to approach them in a scientific and rational way, with a proper objective before us. That kind of approach alone can help us to understand and solve the problems.

I am a socialist because I feel that socialism is a scientific approach to the world's problems. It is not necessary that I should agree with every other socialist but generally a socialist approach is scientific and that appeals to me tremendously. It helps me in understanding the problems of history and history itself. If I try to look at history from a socialist point of view, it helps me to understand the present position because the present has its roots in the past.

Therefore I would like you to consider the various cultural and other problems and apply the scientific approach to your personal life, especially because you are apt to give up this approach in your personal life. When you adopt the scientific approach, you will find a conflict between the personal ideals and the ideals of our public life. This conflict will not, of course, make you happy in your life. But the real joy in life is to work for a great purpose, to understand it, and put all the strength and energy of the integrated mind and personality into its fulfilment. Such an endeavour will give you a sense of fulfilment and real joy.

Selected Works of Jawaharlal Nehru, 1976, IX, pp. 613-17. Address at the cultural conference organized by the students of the Scottish Church College, Calcutta, 3 January 1939. First appeared in *National Herald*, 7 January 1939.

---

* *In the mid-thirties, farmers in the United States of America were granted subsidies for producing less. In 1936, nearly thirty per cent of the total produce of coffee was destroyed, and in England, a quarter of the capacities of the Lancashire mills or ten million cotton spindles were destroyed.*

CHAPTER 11

THE GOOD AND BAD
APPLICATIONS OF SCIENCE

IN my last letter I gave you a peep into the wonderland of the latest developments of science. I do not know if this glimpse will interest you and attract you to these realms of thought and achievement. If you have the desire to know more of these subjects, you can easily find your way to many books. But remember that human thought is ever advancing, ever grappling with and trying to understand the problems of Nature and the universe, and what I tell you today may be wholly insufficient and out-of-date tomorrow. To me there is a great fascination in this challenge of the human mind, and how it soars up to the uttermost corners of the universe and tries to fathom its mysteries, and dares to grasp and measure what appear to be the infinitely big as well as the infinitely small.

All this is what is called 'pure' science – that is, science which has no direct or immediate effect on life. It is obvious that the Theory of Relativity, or the idea of Space-time, or the size of the universe, have nothing to do with our day-to-day lives. Most of these theories depend on higher mathematics, and these intricate and upper regions of mathematics are, in this sense, pure science. Most people are not much interested in this kind of science; they are naturally far more attracted by the applications of science to every-day life. It is this applied science that has revolutionized life during the last 150 years. Indeed, life today is governed and conditioned entirely by these offshoots of science, and it is very difficult for us to imagine existence without them. People often talk about the good old days of the past, of a golden age that is gone. Some periods of past history are singularly attractive, and in some ways they may even have been superior to our time. But even this attraction is probably due more to distance and to a certain vagueness than to anything else, and we are apt to think of an age as being great because of some great men who adorned it and dominated it. The fate of the common people right through history has been a miserable one. Science brought them some relief from their age-long burdens.

Look around you, and you will find that most of the things that you can see are somehow connected with science. We travel by the methods of applied science, we communicate with each other in the same way, our food is often produced that way and carried from one place to another. The newspaper we read could not be produced, nor our books, nor the paper I write on or the pen I write with, by methods other than those of science. Sanitation and health and the conquest over some diseases depend on science. For the modern world it is quite impossible to do without applied science. Apart from all other reasons, one reason is a final and conclusive one: without science there would not be enough food for the world's population, and half of it, or more, would die off from starvation. I have told you how population has gone up with a bound during the last 100 years. This swollen population can only live if the help of science is taken to produce food and transport it from one place to another.

Ever since science introduced the big machine into human life there has been a continuous process of improving it. Innumerable little changes are being made from year to year, and even month to month, which go to make the machine more efficient and less dependent on human labour. These improvements in technique, these advances in technology, as it is called, have become especially rapid during the last thirty years of the twentieth century. The rate of change in recent years—and it is still going on—has been so tremendous, that it is revolutionizing industry and methods of production as much as the Industrial Revolution of the second half of the eighteenth century. This new revolution is largely due to the increasing use of electricity in production. Thus we have had a great Electrical Revolution in the twentieth century, especially in the United States of America, and this is leading to entirely new conditions of life. Just as the Industrial Revolution of the eighteenth century led to the Machine Age, the Electrical Revolution is now leading to the Power Age. Electric power, which is used for industries, railways, and numerous other purposes, dominates everything. It was because of this that Lenin, looking far ahead, decided to build all over Soviet Russia huge hydro-electric power works.

This application of electric power to industry, together with other improvements, often results in a great change without costing much. Thus a slight re-arrangement of electrically-driven machinery might double the production. This is largely due to the progressive elimination of the human factor which is slow and liable to err. Thus, as machines go on improving, fewer workers are employed in them. Huge machines are now controlled by one man handling some levers and switches. This results in increasing the production of manufactured goods enormously, and at the same time throwing out many workers from the factory, as they are no longer required. At the same time advances in technology are so rapid, that, often by the time a new machine is installed in a factory, it is itself partly obsolete because of new improvements.

The process of machines replacing workers had, of course, occurred from the early days of machinery, and, as I think I have told you, there were many riots in those days, and angry workmen broke the new machines. It was found, however, that ultimately machinery resulted in more employment. As a worker could produce far more goods with the help of machinery, his wages went up and the prices of goods went down. The workers and common people could thus buy more of these goods. Their standards of living went up and the demands for manufactured goods grew. This resulted in more factories being built and more men being employed. Thus, although machinery displaced workers in each factory as a whole, far more workers were employed because there were many more factories.

This process went on for a long time, helped as it was by the exploitation by industrial countries of distant markets in backward countries. During the past few years this process seems to have stopped. Perhaps no further expansion is possible umder the present capitalistic system, and some change in the system is necessary. Modern industry goes in for 'mass production', but this can only be carried on if the goods so produced are bought by the masses. If the masses are too poor or are unemployed, then they cannot buy these goods.

In spite of all this, technical improvements go on ceaselessly, and result in machinery displacing men and adding to the unemployed. From 1929 onwards there was a great depression in trade all over the world, but even this did not prevent technology from advancing. It is said that there have been so many improvements *since* 1929 in the United States that millions of people who have been thrown out of work can never be employed, even if the production of 1929 were to be kept up.

This is one of the reasons—there are many others also—that has produced the great problem of the unemployed all over the world, and especially in the advanced industrial countries. It is a curious and inverted problem, for greater production by up-to-date machinery means, or ought to mean, greater wealth for the nation and higher standards of living for every one. Instead, it has resulted in poverty and terrible suffering. One would have thought that a scientific solution of the problem would not be difficult. Perhaps it is not. But the real difficulty comes in trying to solve it scientifically and reasonably. For in doing so many vested interests are affected, and they are powerful enough to control their governments. Then, again, the problem is essentially an international one, and today national rivalries prevent an international solution. Soviet Russia is applying the methods of science to similar problems, but because she has to proceed nationally, the rest of the world being capitalist and hostile to her, she has far greater difficulties than she would otherwise have had. The world is essentially international today, although its political structure lags behind and is narrowly national. For socialism, to succeed finally, it will have to be international world socialism. The hands of the clock cannot be put back, nor can the international structure of today, incomplete as it is, be suppressed in favour of national isolation. An attempt at the intensification of nationalism, as the fascists are trying to do in various countries, is bound to fail in the end, because it runs counter to the fundamental international character of world economy today. It may be, of course, that in so failing it may carry the world with it, and involve what is called modern civilization in a common disaster.

The danger of such a disaster is by no means remote and unthinkable. Science, as we have seen, has brought many good things in its train, but science has also added enormously to the horrors of war. States and governments have often neglected many branches of science, pure and applied. But they have not neglected the warlike aspects of science, and they have taken full advantage of the latest scientific technique to arm and strengthen themselves. Most States rest, in the final analysis, on force, and scientific technique is making these governments so strong that they can tyrannize over people without, as a rule, any fear of consequences. The old days of popular risings against tyrannical governments and the building of barricades and fights in the open streets, such as occurred in the great French Revolution, are long past. It is impossible now for an unarmed or even armed crowd to fight with an organized and well-equipped State force. The State army itself may turn against the Government, as happened in the Russian Revolution, but, unless this happens, it cannot be forcibly defeated. Hence the necesssity has arisen for people, struggling for freedom, to seek other and more peaceful methods of mass action.

Science thus leads to groups or oligarchies controlling States, and to the destruction of individual liberty and the old nineteenth century ideas of democracy. Such oligarchies arise in different States, sometimes outwardly paying homage to the principles of democracy, at other times openly condemning them. These different State oligarchies come into conflict with each other and nations go to war. Such a big war today or in the future may well destroy not only these oligarchies, but civilization itself. Or it may be that out of its ashes an international socialist order might arise, as expected by the Marxist philosophy.

War is not a pleasant subject to contemplate in all its horrid reality, and because of this the reality is hidden behind fine phrases and brave music and bright uniforms. But it is necessary to know something of what war means today. The last war—the World War—brought home to many the horror of war. And yet it is said that the last war was nothing compared to what the next one is likely to be. For if industrial technique has advanced tenfold during the last few years, the science of war has advanced a hundred-fold. War is no longer an affair of infantry charges and cavalry dashes : the old foot-soldier and cavalry man are almost as useless now in war as the bow and arrow. War today is an affair of mechanized tanks (a kind of moving battleship on caterpillar wheels), aeroplanes and bombs, and especially the latter two. Aeroplanes are increasing in speed and efficiency from day to day.

If war breaks out, it is expected that the warring nations will immediately be attacked by hostile aircraft. These aeroplanes will come immediately after the declaration of war, or they may even come before, to steal an advantage over the enemy, and hurl high-explosive bombs at the great cities and factories. Some of the enemy aeroplanes might be destroyed, but the remaining ones will be quite enough to bomb the city. Poison gases will come out of the bombs thrown from aeroplanes, and these will spread and envelop whole areas, suffocating and killing every living thing within their reach. It will be a large-scale destruction of the civilian population in the cruellest and most painful way, causing intolerable suffering and mental distress. And this kind of thing might be done simultaneously in the great cities of the rival Powers at war with each other. In a European war, London, Paris, Berlin might be a heap of smouldering ruins within a few days or weeks.

There is worse to come. The bombs thrown from the aeroplanes might contain germs and bacteria of various horrible diseases, so that a whole city might be infected with these diseases. This kind of 'bacteriological warfare' can be carried on in other ways also : by infecting food and drinking-water and by animal-carriers—for instance, a rat which carries plague.

All this sounds monstrous and incredible, and so it is. Not even a monster would like to do it. But incredible things happen when people are thoroughly afraid and are fighting a life-and-death struggle. The very fear that the enemy country might adopt such unfair and monstrous methods induces each country to be first in the field. For the weapons are so terrible that the country that uses them first has a great advantage. Fear has big eyes !

Indeed, poison gas was used extensively during the last war, and it is well known that all the great Powers have now got large factories to manufacture this gas for war purposes. A curious result of all this is that the real fighting in the next big war will take place not at the front, where some armies might dig themselves in and face each other, but behind the fronts, in the cities and homes of the civilian population. It may even be that the safest place during the war will be the front, for the troops will be fully protected there from air attacks and poison gases and infection ! There will be no such protection for the men left behind, or the women, or the children.

What will be the result of all this ? Universal destruction ? The end of the fine structure of culture and civilization that centuries of effort have built up ?

What will happen no one knows. We cannot tear the veil from the future. We see two processes going on today in the world, two rival and contradictory processes. One is the progress of cooperation and reason, and the building up of the structure of civilization ; the other a destructive process, a tearing up of everything, an attempt by mankind to commit suicide. And both go faster and faster, and both arm themselves with the weapons and technique of science. Which will win ?

Glimpses of World History, 1962, pp. 902-7, Letter dated 14 July 1933 to Indira Gandhi.

CHAPTER 12

WOMEN AND THE FREEDOM MOVEMENT

YESTERDAY a girl asked me what I was going to say at this meeting and at the spur of the moment I said I might advise them not to be too womanly. Then of course I corrected myself by saying that they should not be too womanish. I think that instead of entering into the deep waters of women's representation in the legislatures and the local bodies in the country I would much prefer to talk to you about other and more fundamental matters affecting women. I do not know how many of you have heard the famous saying of a French writer to the effect, that if you want to judge the culture and civilization of a people, you can find that out by the status and condition of the women of the country. You need not look round to see what the men are about, if you find that the women of that country are cultured and civilized and highly advanced in the various walks of life. If the women are backward, that nation is backward. That is, in my opinion, a very important way of judging a nation's advancement.

Many of us in India, as well as elsewhere—because the women's question is not purely an Indian question, although it may concern us here for the time being—are apt to think much more in terms of men who function at the top, who may be advanced and who may be great and forget the part that the women are playing. I should like you, and not only you, because you may take it easily enough, I should like the men of India to apply those scales now and always to the state of affairs in India. What is the condition of the women, what are the women doing, what opening and opportunities have they got, and what disabilities are they labouring under ? If you view the matter from that point of view, inevitably not only will women go up, but the whole nation will go up including the men.

It is pretty obvious that if in a country the population is more or less backward, not advanced, that country cannot go very far. That backward population will drag it down. We are thinking in terms of women without whom it is quite impossible to go ahead.

That applies to many backward classes in the population. If you have large sections—you may call them backward classes, depressed classes, Harijans or economically poor classes—if we have a large proportion of people who have not got opportunities to advance, to go ahead and live normal and natural lives, then that country cannot go very far. You may occasionally produce great men even out of a muddy soil. But the fact remains that you will have to remove the mud before you can have a sane and sober living for the great majority of the people. Therefore whether you look at it from the point of view of women, who have for a long time been the depressed classes in India and in the world, or in terms of other classes of men and women, who are economically and otherwise depressed, we have to remove those bars and give equal opportunity, equal privileges to all of them before we can have an advanced nation.

We are too much in the habit of looking back and praising the past. We are entitled to do that, because there are many things in our past history and culture which are praiseworthy and for which we can take legitimate pride. But that is a bad habit, all the same, to be looking back all the time. In the same way, sometimes I think there is a bit too much talk of Sita and Savitri and the like, estimable ladies no doubt, who played a very brave part and who have become traditional heroines for us. It is right that we should have such heroes and heroines in our national calendar and in our traditions, but we cannot live on tradition alone. Nor can we live on the reputation acquired by ancient heroes and heroines, quite apart from the fact that we cannot entirely apply those examples to modern conditions. Conditions change. While we may take inspiration from the good qualities that the ancient heroes and heroines possessed, we cannot exactly copy everything that might have been done in those times because times have utterly changed.

I said a while ago something about the depressed classes. As a matter of fact, we all, men and women of this country, belong to the depressed classes, because in every country, which is a subject country, the people dominated over inevitably are the depressed and the exploited. Therefore when we talk in terms of getting rid of this exploitation and removing people from their depressed stage to a higher stage, we come across the political problem, and the political problem becomes a common factor for all of us who inhabit this country. Therefore it becomes necessary for all of us to do our utmost and take our part in the struggle for freedom and independence of this country, because so long as that barrier is not removed, I do not think it is possible for us to remove other barriers that keep down women or other depressed groups in the country. I do not mean that we should wait and do nothing at all in regard to the other matters which affect women till India has got political freedom. We have to march together, more or less, on all fronts. But inevitably we cannot go far in any direction till we remove that major barrier of political subjection. Therefore it becomes necessary for the women of India to take their full part in the struggle for political freedom. And apart from that, if they take full part in that — as in a large measure they have done in the past few years — they will reach a stage inevitably in the country, which would make it terribly difficult for their menfolk to be obstructive as before. They would gain a position in the public life of the country from which it would not be possible to remove them.

I do not know very much about the state of affairs during the civil disobedience movement in this province here. But in northern India, where the purdah system has prevailed and many other evil customs of seclusion, the 1930 civil disobedience movement played an extraordinary and astounding part in putting an end to that system of seclusion of women. They came out from their houses when their menfolk were in prison ; they took the lead in the great movement ; they played their part ; they showed quite extraordinary powers of organization, discipline and enterprise. That kind of thing sent up our womenfolk in the estimation of not only our country at large, but of other people in other parts of the world who had been in the habit of saying that Indian women were slaves and incapable of doing anything. They were surprised and astounded at the change that they saw.

So therefore women should take the fullest part in the political struggle for freedom, political and economic. But remember that politics and economics are after all a means to an end. Even political independence, important as it is, is only a means to a certain end. What are the fundamental questions that people have to face all over the world ? These could be resolved into the relation of man to man, man to woman and man to society.

Probably all things will come under these heads, and when we consider these wider and larger questions, the political side is not quite so important as it might otherwise appear to be. We in India inevitably are somewhat overwhelmed by the political aspect of the matter, because that happens to be a tremendous barrier in our way. And so long as that barrier is not removed, we can think of little else; yet, so far as women are concerned you cannot think entirely on this political plane. You have to think also on your own plane and think of your own disabilities, because you are not likely to be helped by your menfolk. Therefore whilst you will have to share with men in the struggle for political freedom, you will have to bear the whole burden of the struggle for women's emancipation yourself. And the sooner you realize that the better will it be for you. Individuals may sympathize with you; individuals may also help you. But still you will have to fight, not so much perhaps actual opposition, although of that there will be enough, but tremendous inertia which is far more dangerous to combat. You will have, if you want to combat it, to go on with all your strength all the time, because the moment you sit down, the inertia overwhelms you and puts an end to your work. I am glad I see evidence of this activity to some extent, though not enough. Women's movements are rising up, trying for the removal of various disabilities and seeking representation of women in all political bodies. It is essential that women should have a voice because they will not only be helpful but also reasonable, sensible and peaceful. There is one danger against which I would like to warn you and that is this; that in your desire to fight against the disabilities, you might forget the political struggle. Today the principal urge in India is the nationalist urge for political freedom and for economic freedom. Both these are common for men and women and if you try to function outside these two urges and cut yourself adrift from the living current of national life, your movement will be functioning in the air, and you will be functioning in little coteries and drawing-room parties.

Your president has referred to the part that women should take in the various bodies and committees, political and other, in the country. I entirely agree with her. As I have already said, apart from the necessity of women having to consider the major issues, it is quite absurd that that alone should be the work. So far as the

Congress is concerned I should very much like, I would welcome, more and more women occupying prominent positions in committees and boards and its executives. So far as the Congress constitution is concerned, it not only welcomes but encourages women to come in. There are not very many women at the present moment occupying seats of authority in the Congress Party; that may be due, unfortunately, to the fact that men do not like pushing women ahead and you have to face that also. If the women ask and are really keen about it and push ahead, you are bound to get it because there is a strong body of public opinion behind you. Men also would welcome this. I hope that your push will have such strength that it will become very difficult for men to refuse your demands. I thank you once again for your welcome.

Selected Works of Jawaharlal Nehru, 1975, VII, pp. 479-83. Speech delivered in Madras, 6 October 1936. First appeared in *The Hindu* (evening edition), 6 October 1936.

CHAPTER 13

THE LITERATURES OF INDIA

I AM a little embarrassed in having to address you, and I feel like an outsider who has strayed into distinguished company. You have done me the honour of making me a Vice President of the Indian Centre of the P.E.N., and I deem it a privilege. But you know very well that my work has been in another direction, and that other activities have absorbed my attention far too much. I am not untouched by, as Sir Mirza put it, 'the spiritual paralysis of politics'. And yet I have sometimes strayed into other fields by accident, queer and incidental. By accident I became a writer, and so found my way into the P.E.N.

So far as this subject is concerned, I am quite sure that many of you who are present here know much more about it than I do, and could do more justice to it. All I can say is of a very general nature, and perhaps that will be an advantage, because that will mean that I will not inflict myself for too long a time on you. The subject is : 'The Development of the Indian Literatures as a Uniting Force'. It is a fascinating subject, and I wish I knew more about it except that there is so much to know if one really is to deal with it in any proper style, which is truly beyond me.

The questions that strike me in this connection are these: Are Indian literatures a uniting force or not? Do we take it for granted that they are a uniting force or that they are going to be a uniting force? A superficial survey would, I am afraid, tend to show that they create or might create greater provincialism and erect new barriers to unity. As you know, one of the questions to which frequent reference is made nowadays is the so-called 'language question' of India. When we talk about the 'language question', we do not refer to the dozen or so languages—the principal languages—of India, but rather to Hindi and Urdu, which are one language with different literary forms drawing inspiration from the same fountain-head. That is the language question! There is hardly any cause, so far as I know, for any conflict between the different languages in their different spheres; but conflict appears sometimes with regard to Hindi or Urdu, though they are but one language with different literary forms.

However, it is interesting to trace the development of Indian languages. For long centuries, they formed a happy joint family, very much dependent on their parent language, Sanskrit—so dependent indeed that they did not grow at all. Later, Persian came into the field, superficially on the top. Persian also affected our languages, but it was a restraining force which would not allow them to grow, since learned people then thought it beneath their dignity to write or speak at select assemblies like this in any language but Sanskrit or Persian. If anything worthwhile was to be written, surely it must be written in Sanskrit, not in Hindi or Bengali or some other dialect; and to some extent that happened later with regard to Persian. People talked or wrote in Sanskrit or Persian. Of course, only a very small circle could talk in those languages, and that is why, I suppose, this divorce between that small circle at the top talking or writing in Sanskrit or Persian and the vast numbers talking in other languages, more living languages, prevented the growth of these latter, and the growth also of our modern literatures.

Now when I say that Sanskrit and Persian were a restraining influence, please do not imagine that I am condemning Sanskrit or Persian at all. Sanskrit is of course something of which every Indian is infinitely and rightly proud. Sanskrit really has performed a great unifying task throughout the ages, and as a unifying force it has obviously been the greatest instrument of the continuity of our culture for thousands of years. There is therefore no question whatever of my condemning Sanskrit.

Persian came late in the field of development of the Indian languages, and yet it played a fairly important part in later centuries, affecting almost all our provincial languages considerably—and thus Persian too became a part of our national heritage. In this way Persian also became a unifying force, at any rate for the upper classes, though not so much for the masses.

Sanskrit, then, pre-eminently, and Persian to some extent, have played a great part in Indian literary life. For my part, I would like large numbers of persons all over India to study Sanskrit, and also Persian, because it is a very beautiful language and is intimately associated, not only with our modern languages but with

Sanskrit, which, as you know, is its sister language. Hindi, in fact, is nearer to Persian in some respects than to classical Sanskrit.

However that may be, the fact we should remember is that our provincial languages were controlled by these two aristocratic languages, by Sanskrit especially ; and it took a tremendous lot of time for the povincial languages to grow. Gradually, by force of circumstances, out of the hundreds of original dialects, Hindi developed, Bengali developed, Marathi and Gujarati and other languages developed. In the South, of course, there was a different family of languages, which, though different, became through Sanskrit intimately associated with the other languages of India—and so we have now about a dozen principal languages of India.

One of the remarkable instances of the development of languages in India is provided by Urdu, which grew up and exhibited the interplay of these various forces that flowed in India during the last two hundred years, and became essentially an Indian language, with probably 80 per cent of words that are common to it and Hindi, but of course with a number of Persian words as well. The main difference between Hindi and Urdu is not so much in the vocabulary but in their respective literary forms. The Hindi literary form has been, I suppose, derived directly from Sanskrit—I speak with diffidence in this matter—and all the metaphors and similes and ways of thought and expression have been likewise derived from Sanskrit, and also from the common background of life in India. Thus the literary and other forms of Hindi are Indian no doubt, for no outside influence has permeated them, but they are very old, and long after they have ceased to have any meaning, some of them are still being used.

Urdu, the same language as Hindi with almost the same vocabulary, with a few words thrown in from outside, developed as an entirely different literary form. Its ways of expression were not derived from Indian life as a rule ; its similes and metaphors were derived from Central Asia, or the Caucasus or Iran, and today in our colloquial Hindustani or Hindi so many of these expressions, similes and metaphors, which are not really Indian in origin, have become very common.

As I have said already, the language question mainly deals with Hindi and Urdu. Why there should be so much argument and so much heat and passion, I do not know. But, of course, it is now hardly a question of language. It has become a question of selection of a common language for India, and that is why, perhaps, there is so much heat and passion. It has become a political question in a way, or rather, in a way politics affects the question very much.

The result is obvious. In Hindi and Urdu we have formed certain literary devices, or have certain sophisticated patterns, which attract those who are orthodox. But these devices and patterns have lost their vitality or popular appeal, and must progressively grow more and more stale in spite of a certain beauty in them, because those forms are wholly unconnected with the life of the common people. They remain the same, oblivious to the changing environment. That, of course, applies not only to Hindi and Urdu but to so many aspects of our life. We are sticking to ancient forms so much in our social life, sometimes without any perceptible sense in those forms, that some of our activities are a puzzle even to people just outside our province in our own country. And language, after all, is something which reflects the life of the people. If the life of the people is confined to a narrow circle of old-fashioned forms, then inevitably their language also is bound to be like that. And it is no use blaming the standard of this or that language, if that language became isolated from the life of the people. I refer only to the literary language, because the popular languages of this time revealed their vitality in popular songs, folk songs, and the rest. Though these popular songs were quite vital in their own way, they had no chance of gaining importance in the centres of learned people for, say, a hundred years. In our popular languages we find folk songs, balads, poems, etc, while the prose works were limited to Sanskrit or Persian. But the popular languages flourished among the common people and in the households. So this divorce between the language of the common people and the language of the learned persons has had, I suppose, a very harmful effect on the growth of our languages. That divorce, in a sense, has had its harmful effect, not only on those languages, but on life itself. Many of our ills in India, I think, are probably the result of that. Well, anyhow these popular languages grew, in spite of all the obstructions and the various influences restricting their growth, because life has to grow. But they grew so slowly, and in fact much of their growth has taken place in poetry, in which some of our languages are very rich. Almost all the growth of these our Indian languages has taken place during the last two hundred years or less — here, again, I am subject to correction — and especially their literatures are of recent growth.

Now the growth of these provincial languages has not, so far as I know, tended at all towards disunity. To some extent, no doubt, it may have accentuated a certain provincialism, or given a little push to provincial culture. A Bengali is very rightly proud of his Bengali language, Gujaratis of their Gujarati, Maharashtrians of Marathi, and so on. They have their legitimate prides, but I do not think that there is any conflict between this feeling and the larger feeling of national identity, because the whole basis of India's thought, as I know it, has been never a mere regimentation of people's ideas, but of unity plus diversity, plus variety. Therefore the two do not conflict, because each province, each linguistic area, taking pride in its own past cultural achievements, realizes that it is but part of a larger whole. In the past, the cultural unity of India was maintained, not only by one language, Sanskrit, but also by a special philosophy which was common to the whole of India. The old philosophical outlook was later on superseded to some extent at least, and therefore I feel that it is not now strong enough to be a unifying force to the extent, to the degree, it was in the past. Other things have happened. Possibly, the unifying force today would be, not so much national but something more international, something which is common to all nations, — which, again, would not mean the submergence of the national identity in its entirety, but rather the two existing together.

I do not personally see any need to answer the questions which I put at the beginning I do not see anything tending towards disunity or towards real essential separatism in the growth of provincial languages in India. There is also another factor to consider. In fact, if I may quote the instance of Rabindranath Tagore, it is extraordinary how a man like Tagore who wrote in the Bengali language influenced every other language in India. Hindi certainly, and also the other languages. It shows how these cultural giants grow across provincial barriers. If one language grows, it surely helps others to grow. It does not hinder the others. It does not come into conflict with them. That is my chief grievance with those people who fight and argue about Hindi and Urdu. I have no doubt in my mind that if Hindi grows rich it will help Urdu, and if Urdu grows rich it will help Hindi.

I am quite sure at the same time that Hindi and Urdu are bound to grow nearer to each other, not because you and I may like it or not like it, but because circumstances are forcing us to develop them as a common language. It seems to me a sheer waste of energy that these champions of Urdu should so strongly object to Hindi influence, and vice versa.

Therefore, I do feel that this renaissance of our provincial languages that has taken place is a thing which helps towards unification, and can never be a destructive factor in India. But apart from the language question, it depends again on the background of politics as they develop in India, because languages will be affected by them. For example, there is the Pakistan controversy. Suppose, for a moment, that Urdu becomes the official language in Pakistan and Hindi in the rest of India. If that leads to the destruction of Indian unity, it is not the fault of the language but of certain arguments on the political front that are taking place in India. Languages by themselves, I am convinced, are not a destructive factor, not at all a factor leading to disunity, partly because the languages are akin to each other and the growth of one helps to build up the others, and anyhow they are not going to hinder each other's growth.

Apart from this question of politics behind them, ultimately it all depends mainly on whether we have some kind of a common philosophy, common ethical standards, common artistic standards. If they differ greatly, then those divergences may show themselves in our languages and may lead to unfortunate consequences. If there are vital differences or fundamental differences in our philosophy of life, then the barriers between nations will remain high. If we have certain standards of conduct in common, we can get along amicably, even if we may differ physically, spiritually and artistically. If not, I can only guess what the future is going to be. I am not quite competent to know for certain which will triumph, the good in life or the evil in life.

One thing more before I finish my half hour, and that is this : in literature everything depends on how much freedom there is to function. Freedom of thought, freedom of expression, freedom of occupation, and freedom generally to function as we believe, are all essential for the growth of literature. The slowness in the development of many of our languages is largely due to the absence of political freedom. Lack of political freedom comes in the way of all progress. But even in a politically free India, if there is no freedom of speech and expression, then it can only be an obstruction in the way of the growth of our languages and it may even lead to unhealthy and disuniting forces growing up. Restrictions on freedom of speech and expression will prevent the languages from affecting the minds of the people at large. That means that you are creating barriers to their self-expression, that you are separating some people at the top from the vast masses at the bottom and thereby creating a select coterie which functions in an artificial atmosphere. There is nothing more dangerous than this idea of authority. Personally, I rebel against that idea in all its phases. In this connection, I was surprised at the whole body of the P.E.N. standing up when a princely message was read this morning, even though it may be in accordance with the traditions of the State.

So it seems to me that the very essence of our growth is this essential freedom, political freedom, because the other types of freedom depend on this. Along with political freedom, there must of course be freedom of speech and expression. Also, the words that we use, the language that we use, should keep in touch with changing conditions. We are a conservative people and we still stick to false values. This sticking to outmoded values obstructs the growth of one's culture. It has already done us immense harm. Sanskrit lost its popularity because it did not keep in touch with the life of the people. One reason why provincial languages and literatures are more vital today than they were before is because they went back to the life of the people and drew inspiration from it. That, again, is another reason why they should develop as a uniting force, because the life of the people in India, taken as a whole, does not differ greatly. The difference—such as it is—is at the top. If you once go down to the large masses, you come to something that is common,—whether you express it in this language or in that language does not matter.

Well, now I leave it to more learned persons to continue this discussion.

Selected Works of Jawaharlal Nehru, 1981, XIV, pp. 603-9. Speech delivered at the first All-India Writers' Conference, Jaipur, 20 October 1945. First published in *Indian Writers in Council* by P.E.N. Centre, Bombay.

CHAPTER 14

SOME FAMOUS WRITERS

AS I was writing to you yesterday about the rise of Germany, it struck me that I had not told you anything about the greatest German of the early nineteenth century. This man was Goethe, a famous writer, the centenary of whose death was celebrated all over Germany a few months ago. And then I thought that I might tell you something about the famous writers of this period in Europe. But this was a dangerous subject for me, dangerous because I would only show my own ignorance. Just to give a list of well-known names would be rather silly, and to say something more would be difficult. I know little enough about English literature, and of the other European literatures my knowledge is confined to a few translations. What, then, was I to do?

The idea to say something on the subject had taken possession of my mind, and I could not rid myself of it. I felt that I should at least point out this direction to you, even though I cannot accompany you far along the way to this enchanted land. For art and literature often give greater insight into a nation's soul than the superficial activities of the multitude. They take us to a region of calm and serene thought which is not affected by the passions and prejudices of the moment. But today the poet and the artist are seldom looked upon as the prophets of tomorrow and they meet with little honour. If some honour comes to them at all, it usually comes after they are dead.

So I shall mention just a few names to you, some of which must be already familiar to you, and I shall only touch upon the early part of the century. This is just to whet your appetite. Remember that the nineteenth century has rich stores of fine writing in many of the European countries.

Goethe really belonged to the eighteenth century, for he was born in 1749, but he lived to the ripe old age of eighty-three, and thus saw a good third of the next century. He lived through one of the stormiest periods of European history, and saw his own country overrun by Napoleon's armies. In his own life he experienced much sorrow, but gradually he gained an inner command over life's difficulties and attained a detachment and calm which brought peace to him. Napoleon first saw him when he was over sixty. As he stood in the doorway, there was something in his face and figure, an untroubled look and a bearing so full of dignity, that Napoleon exclaimed: 'Voila un homme!' He dabbled in many things, and whatever he did, he did with distinction. He was a philosopher, a poet, a dramatist, and a scientist interested in many different sciences, and, besides all this, his practical job was that of a minister in the Court of a petty German prince! He is best known to us as a writer, and his most famous book is *Faust*. His fame spread far during his long life, and in his own sphere of literature he came to be regarded by his countrymen almost as a demi-god.

Goethe had a contemporary, somewhat younger than he was, named Schiller, who was also a great poet. Much younger was Heinrich Heine, yet another great and delightful poet in German, who has written very beautiful lyrics. All these three—Goethe, Schiller and Heine—were steeped in the classical culture of ancient Greece.

Germany has long been known as the land of philosophers, and I might as well mention one or two names to you, although perhaps they will not interest you greatly. Only those people who have a passion for the subject need try to read their books, for they are very abstruse and difficult. None the less these and other philosophers are interesting and instructive, for they kept alight the torch of thought, and through them one can follow the development of ideas. Immanuel Kant was the great German philosopher of the eighteenth century, and he lived on to the turn of the century, when he was eighty. Hegel is another great name in philosophy. He followed Kant, and is supposed to have greatly influenced Karl Marx, the father of communism. So much for the philosophers.

The early years of the nineteenth century produced quite a number of eminent poets, especially in England. Russia's best-known national poet, Pushkin, also lived then. He died young as the result of a duel. There were several poets in France also, but I shall mention only two French names. One is that of Victor Hugo, who was born in 1802 and lived, like Goethe, to the age of eighty-three and, also like Goethe, became a kind of demi-god of literature in his own country. He had a varied career both as a writer and as a politician. He started life as an aggressive royalist and almost a believer in autocracy. Gradually he changed step by step till he became a republican in 1848. Louis Napoleon, when he became President of the short-lived Second Republic, exiled him for his republican views. In 1871 Victor Hugo favoured the Commune of Paris. From the extreme right of conservatism he had moved gradually but surely to the extreme left of socialism. Most people grow conservative and reactionary as they become older. Hugo did the exact opposite. But we are concerned here with him as a writer. He was a greater poet, novelist and dramatist.

The second French name I shall mention to you is that of Honoré de Balzac. He was a contemporary of Victor Hugo's, but was very different from him. He was a novelist of tremendous energy, and wrote a huge number of novels during a fairly short life. His stories are connected with one another; the same characters often appear in them. His object was to mirror the whole of the French life of his day in his novels, and he called the whole series *La Comedie Humaine*. It was a very ambitious idea, and although he worked hard and long, he could not complete the enormous task he had set himself.

In England three brilliant young poets stand out in the early years of the nineteenth century. They were contemporaries, and they all died young within three years of each other. These three were Keats, Shelley and Byron. Keats had a hard tussle with poverty and discouragement, and when he died in Rome in 1821 at the age of twenty-six he was little known. And yet he had written some very beautiful poetry. Keats belonged to the middle classes, and it is interesting to note that if lack of money was an obstruction in his way, how much more difficult must it be for the poor to become poets and writers. Indeed, the present Cambridge Professor of English Literature has some pertinent remarks to make about this:

'It is,' he says, 'certain that, by some fault in our commonwealth, the poor poet has not in these days, nor has had for two hundred years, a dog's chance. Believe me—and I have spent a great part of ten years in watching some three hundred and twenty elementary schools,—we may prate of democracy, but actually, a poor child in England has little more hope than had the son of an Athenian slave to be emancipated into that intellectual freedom of which great writings are born.'

I have given this quotation because we are apt to forget that poetry and fine writing, and culture generally, are monopolies of the well-to-do classes. Poetry and culture have little place in a poor man's hut; they are not meant for empty stomachs. So our present-day culture becomes a reflection of the well-to-do *bourgeois* mind. It may change greatly when the worker takes charge of it in a different social system where he has the opportunities and leisure to indulge in culture. Some such change is being watched with interest in Soviet Russia today.

This also makes it clear to us that a great deal of our cultural poverty in India during the last few generations is due to our people's excessive poverty. It is an insult to talk of culture to people who have nothing to eat. This blight of poverty affects even those few who happen to be relatively well-to-do, and so unhappily even these classes in India are today singularly uncultured. What a host of evils foreign rule and social backwardness have to answer for. But even in this general poverty and drabness, India can still produce splendid men and magnificent exemplars of culture like Gandhi and Rabindranath Tagore.

I have drifted away from my subject.

Shelley was a most lovable creature; full of fire from his early youth and the champion of freedom in everything. He was expelled from his college at Oxford for writing an essay on *The Necessity of Atheism*. He (and Keats also) went through his brief life as a poet is supposed to do, living in his imagination and in the air and regardless of worldly difficulties. He was drowned near the Italian coast a year after the death of Keats. I need not tell you of his famous poems as you can easily find them out for yourself. But I shall give you one of his shorter poems. It is by no means among his best, but it brings out the awful fate of the poor worker in our present civilization. He is in almost as bad a condition as the old slaves were. It is more than 100 years since the poem was written, and yet it applies to present-day conditions. It is called *The Mask of Anarchy*.

What is Freedom?—ye can tell
That which slavery is, too well—
For its very name has grown
To an echo of your own.

'Tis to work and have such pay
As just keeps life from day to day
In your limbs, as in a cell
For the tyrant's use to dwell.

So that ye for them are made
Loom, and plough, and sword, and spade,
With or without your own will bent
To their defence and nourishment.

'Tis to see your children weak
With their mothers pine and peak,
When the winter winds are bleak—
They are dying, whilst I speak.

'Tis to hunger for such diet
As the rich man in his riot
Casts to the fat dogs that lie
Surfeiting beneath his eye.

'Tis to be a slave in soul
And to hold no strong control
Over your own wills, but be
All that others make of ye.

And at length, when ye complain
With a murmur weak and vain,
'Tis to see that tyrant's crew
Ride over your wives and you—
Blood is on the grass like dew.

Byron has also written fine poetry in praise of freedom, but it is
national freedom, and not economic freedom, as in Shelley's
poem. He died, as I have told you, in the Greek national war of

liberation against Turkey, two years after Shelley. I am rather prejudiced against Byron as a man, and yet I have a fellow-feeling for him, for did he not go to Harrow School and Trinity College, Cambridge—my school and college? Unlike Keats and Shelley, fame came to him in his youth, and he was lionized by London society only to be dropped later.

There were two other well-known poets about this time, both much longer-lived than this youthful trio. Wordsworth, who lived for eighty years from 1770 to 1850, is considered one of the great English poets. He was very fond of Nature, and much of his poetry is Nature-poetry. The other was Coleridge; a few of his poems are very good.

The early nineteenth century also saw three famous novelists. Walter Scott was the eldest of these, and his Waverley novels were very popular. I suppose you have read some of them. I remember liking them when I was a boy, but tastes change as one grows up, and I am sure they would bore me now if I read them. Thackeray and Dickens were the two other novelists. Both, I think, are far superior to Scott. I hope they are both friends of yours. Thackeray was born in Calcutta in 1811, and spent five or six years there. Some of his books have got realistic descriptions of the Indian nabobs—that is, the English people in India who, having collected a huge fortune and become fat and peppery, returned to England to enjoy themselves.

This is as much as I propose to write about the writers of the early nineteenth century. It is ridiculously little about a big subject. A person who knows the subject could write charmingly about it; he would also, no doubt, tell you a lot about the music and art of the period. All this requires telling and knowing, but they are beyond me, and I shall wisely keep to solid ground.

I shall finish up this letter by giving you a poem from Goethe's *Faust*. This is, of course, a translation from the German:

> Alas, alas!
>> Thou hast smitten the world,
>> Thou hast laid it low.
> Shattered, o'er thrown,
>> Into nothingness hurled
>> Crushed by a demi-god's blow.

We bear them away,
   The shards of the world.
We sing well-a-day
   Over the loveliness gone,
   Over the beauty slain.
Build it again,
   Great child of Earth,
Build it again
   With a finer worth,
In thine own bosom build it on high!
   Take up thy life once more:
Run the race again!
   High and clear
Let a lovelier strain
   Ring out than ever before!

Glimpses of World History, 1962, pp. 534-38. Letter dated 1 February 1933 to Indira Gandhi.

CHAPTER 15

ON EDUCATION

WHEN your friendly invitation to inaugurate this Conference reached me by telephone at Wardha, I hesitated for a moment, but for a moment only, for one may not dally with a long-distance call. I felt honoured that a body of learned men should have summoned me to their select gathering. For though I have not been a stranger to the halls of learning, for many years my path branched off from them and took me to strange and dusty byways. Often I had dipped into those wells where lie imprisoned the thoughts and dreams and experiences of past ages, but fate and circumstances conspired together to drag me away from that pleasant and ordered life and cast my lot among the vast unlearned of this country. I met multitudes of men and women, the vast majority of whom had never known school or college, nor had they ever been touched in any way by the education that the state or private enterprise had organized.

I felt attracted by your invitation for what is there more attractive and vital today than education? In this warring world, full of sorrow and conflict, with a thousand problems oppressing us, how shall we find peace and a solution for these problems except through right education ?

So I have come to you to wish you well and to commend your labours. It would ill become me, a layman and an amateur, to discuss the intricate problems which are meant for experts. But there is danger in the expert's specialized way of looking at things, for he may lose the right perspective and forget to see life as a whole. That danger has to be guarded against especially now when the very foundations of life are challenged and are at stake. What is your objective, your aim in education ? Surely you train the rising generation for life. What pattern of life do you envisage, for unless you have that clear picture in your minds, the education that you give will be superficial, faulty and aimless, and your problems and difficulties will ever increase. You will go on lecturing on navigation while the ship is going down.

The ideal of education has long been the improvement of the

individual. That ideal must inevitably hold, for without individual advancement there can be no social progress. But even that care of the individual must today be considered in terms of the mass of the people or else the enlightened individual will be submerged in the unenlightened mass. And, in any event, is it right or just that a group of individuals should have opportunities of advancement and growth which are denied to the many ?

But, even from the standpoint of the individual, a vital question has to be faced. Can an individual truly advance, except in the rarest cases, if the environment that surrounds him is pulling him back all the time ? If this environment is evil or injurious to him, the individual battles in vain against it and must inevitably be crushed by it. What is this environment ? It consists of inherited ideas, prejudices and superstitions which restrict the mind and prevent growth and change in a changing world. It is the pressure of political circumstances that keeps the individual and the group in enforced subjection and thus starves his soul and crushes his spirit. It is, above all, the stranglehold of economic conditions which denies opportunity to vast masses of people. It is this complex of prejudice and superstition, political and economic conditions, that form our environment which holds us in its grip.

Through your educational system you may teach all the well-known virtues, but life today teaches something else, and the voice of life is louder and more effective. You may teach the advantages of cooperative effort, but our social structure is based on cut-throat competition, and each one tries to rise on the dead selves of others. The glittering prizes go to him who is most successful in knocking down and crushing his rivals. Is it any wonder that our youth should be attracted by these glittering prizes, and should hold acquisitiveness as the most desirable quality in an acquisitive society ?

We swear by nonviolence in this country, yet violence envelops us not only in its more obvious forms of warring nations but in the very social structure in which we live. Out of this violent environment no real peace or nonviolence can ever come, unless we change that environment itself.

Our educational system, in spite of the ideals which it may profess, is itself an outcome of and a part of this environment. It seeks sustenance from it and, consciously or unconsciously, supports it. Yet if there is anything clear in the world today, it is this : that this environment is the cause of most of our troubles, and to leave it as it is, is to head straight for disaster.

Indeed, it may already be too late to prevent that disaster, and the war that is raging in Europe may yet shatter the edifice of modern civilization. We shall not escape this tragedy, and even if we survive this general collapse our own problems threaten to overwhelm us, unless we see aright and act aright. Recent events have shown how strong the forces of evil and disruption and narrow-minded bigotry are in this country. We have seen also how the dominant political and economic interests resent and combat change.

These are larger problems which will not come up before this Conference, and yet they affect our education vitally and all our educational efforts will be in vain if these problems do not find proper and early solution. But even apart from the problems of the moment, no educationist can ignore the vital question of what education should aim at in the social and economic sphere. All education must have a definite social outlook and must train our youth for the kind of society we wish to have. Politicians may strive for political and economic changes in order to bring that society into existence, but the real basis of that society must be laid in the teaching of our schools and colleges. The real change will have to come in the minds of men, though that change can and will be helped greatly by external changes in the environment. The two processes go together and should help each other.

Our present-day social fabric is a decadent and dying thing, full of its own contradictions, and leading continually to war and conflict. This acquisitive and competitive society must be ended and must give place to a cooperative order, where we think in terms not of individual profit but of the common good; where individuals cooperate with each other and nations and peoples work in cooperation for human advancement; where human values count for more and there is no exploitation of a class or group or nation by another.

If this is the accepted ideal of our future society then all our education must be fashioned to that end and must not pay homage to anything that is against this conception of the social order. That education will always have to think in terms of the hundreds of millions of our people, and not sacrifice their interests for any group or class. The teacher will then be not just a follower of a profession which gives him a livelihood, but one who has chosen his vocation in the ardent spirit of a missionary in a sacred cause which fills his being.

Recently much thought has been given in India to educational progress and people's minds are astir and expectant and full of hope in this world of today which has so little hope. You will no doubt consider the new Basic Scheme of education. The more I have studied this and watched it grow, the more fascinated I have been by it. Further experience will no doubt bring changes and variations but I have little doubt that we have found in this scheme the path that leads to mass education on the right lines, when education keeps in tune with life and prepares for life. Particularly it is suited to a poor country like India.

As I have wandered about India and seen her millions of unhappy, sorrow-laden people, with sunken eyes and hopeless look, I have felt overwhelmed with the tragedy of India. Yet I have always sensed the tremendous vitality of our people and felt confident that they will pull themselves out of this miserable condition and recover the bright and happy faces and hopeful eyes that should be the birthright of every individual. They hunger and have not the wherewithal to eat, they seek work and find none, their bare bodies shiver in the cold, their homes are mud huts, continually tumbling down, bright-eyed opportunity never comes their way.

All this is tragedy and must be remedied. But the greatest tragedy is the killing of the spirit, when there is no hope or sense of adventure or pride left in them. It is this that we have to end before India is reborn.

> Let not young souls be smothered out before
> They do quaint deeds and fully flaunt their pride,
> It is the world's one crime its babes grow dull,
> Its poor are ox-like, limp and leaden-eyed.
> Not that they starve, but starve so dreamlessly,
> Not that they sow, but that they seldom reap,
> Not that they serve, but have no gods to serve,
> Not that they die but that they die like sheep.

It is pleasant for intellectual and enlightened people to discuss calmly the affairs of a troubled and distant world. They feel secure and well-contented in their limited spheres, cut off from reality. But reality is upon us now and the troubled world is no longer distant but threatens to envelop and overwhelm us. Those who are frightened of this unpleasant reality and seek refuge from it, struggle helplessly and bitterly against fate, and function more and more like marionettes controlled by unseen forces. None of us dare to act in this weak ineffectual way when everything that is worthwhile in life calls to us to clear thought and brave deeds. The world is unpleasant; let us realize it and then, like men, seek to change it and make it a pleasanter, juster place for all of us to live in.

Selected Works of Jawaharlal Nehru, 1977, X, pp. 598-601. Inaugural address at the All-India Educational Conference, Baradari, 27 December 1939. First appeared in *National Herald*, 28 December 1939.

CHAPTER 16

STUDENTS AND POLITICS

INDIA at present is a peculiar country and the questions that are raised surprise one. Some even argue that the independence of India is bad for India; that something less than independence is in reality more than it. Not being metaphysically inclined I find some difficulty in understanding these abstruse problems. Yet another peculiar question relates to students and politics. Students must not take part in politics, some say. What is politics ? According to the usual interpretation in India (official India), to assist or support the government in any way is not politics; but it is politics to criticize or work against the existing order in India.

Who are the students ? They may be children in the elementary schools or young men and women in colleges. Obviously the same considerations cannot apply to both.

Quite a large number of senior students today possess a vote for the coming provincial elections. To vote is to take part in politics; to vote intelligently necessitates the understanding of political issues; to understand political issues results usually in accepting a certain political policy; and if one accepts that policy it is the duty of the citizen to push that policy, to try to convert others to it. Thus inevitably a voter must be a politician, and he should be an ardent politician if he is a keen citizen. Only those who lack the political or social sense can remain passive and neutral or indifferent.

Even apart from his duty as a voter, every student must, if he is properly trained, prepare himself for life and its problems. Otherwise his education has been wasted effort. Politics and economics deal with these problems and no person is properly educated unless he understands them. Perhaps it is difficult for most people to see a clear path through life's jungle. But whether we know the solution of the problem or not, we must at least know the nature of it. What are the questions that life puts to us ? The answers may be difficult, but the curious thing is that people seek to answer without knowing the real questions. No serious or thinking student can take up this futile attitude.

The various *isms* that play such an important part in the world today—nationalism, liberalism, socialism, communism, imperialism, fascism, etc.—are efforts on the part of various groups to answer these questions. Which answer is correct ? Or are they all steeped in error ? In any event we have to choose and in order to choose we must know and have the capacity to choose correctly. This cannot be done if there are repressions and suppressions of thought and action. It cannot be done properly if High Authority sits on us and prevents the free play of the mind.

Thus it becomes necessary for all thinking individuals, and more so for the student than for others, to take the fullest theoretical part in politics. Naturally this will apply to the senior students at life's threshold rather than the junior ones who are still far from these problems. But a theoretical consideration is not enough for a proper understanding; even theory requires practice. From the point of view of study alone the student must leave his lecture halls and investigate reality in village and town, in field and factory; to take part to some extent in the various activities of the people, including political activities.

One has ordinarily to draw the line somewhere. A student's first business is to train his mind and body and make them efficient instruments for thought, understanding and action. Before he is trained he cannot think or act effectively. Yet the training itself comes not from listening to pious advice, but by indulging in action to some extent. That action, under normal conditions, must be subordinated to the theoretical training. But it cannot be eliminated or else the training itself is deficient.

It is our misfortune that in India our educational system is thoroughly lopsided. But an even greater misfortune is the highly authoritarian atmosphere that surrounds it. Not in education alone, but everywhere in India, red-liveried, pompous and often empty-headed Authority seeks to mould people after its own pattern and prevent the growth of the mind and the spread of ideas. Recently we have seen how this Authority has made a mess of things even in the realm of sport and our cricket team in England, full of brilliant players, was effectively hamstrung by the ignorant nobodies who controlled it.* Genius was sacrificed so that Authority might triumph. In our universities this spirit of

In June 1936 the famous cricketer Amarnath was expelled from the Indian team touring England by its manager Brittain Jones as a 'disciplinary measure'.

authority reigns supreme and, in the name of discipline, comes down heavily on any who do not meekly obey. They do not like the qualities that are encouraged in free countries, the spirit of daring, the adventures of the soul in uncharted regions. Is it surprising then that we do not produce many men and women who seek to conquer the Poles or Everest, to control the elements and bring them to man's use, to hurl defiance at man's ignorance and timidity and inertia and littleness and try to raise him up to the stars ?

Must students take part in politics ? Must they take part in life, a full wholesome part in life's varied activities, or be of the clerkly breed, carrying out orders from above ? As students they cannot keep out of politics, as Indian students even more so they must keep in touch with them. Yet it is true that normally the training of their minds and bodies must be their principal consideration during this period of their growth. They must observe a certain discipline but that discipline should not be such as crushes the mind and kills the spirit.

So, normally. But abnormal conditions come when all normal rules are swept away. During the Great War where were the students of England, France, Germany ? Not in their colleges but in the trenches, facing and meeting death. Where are the students of Spain today ?

A subject country is always to some extent in an abnormal condition. So India is today. And in considering these problems we must also consider our environment and the growing abnormality in the world. And as we seek to understand it; we are driven to take part, however little it might be, in the shaping of events.

Selected Works of Jawaharlal Nehru, 1975, VII, pp. 475-77. Speech delivered in Allahabad, 1 October 1936. First published in the *Students' Tribune*, Lahore and reprinted in *Eighteen Months in India*, (Allahabad, 1938), pp. 51-55.

CHAPTER 17

COTTAGE AND LARGE-SCALE INDUSTRIES

I HAVE been asked to speak on cottage industry. Cottage industry is an important problem but there are problems more important than cottage industry. These problems are affecting the whole world and if we are not prepared to face them they will crush us.

I am not a war-monger nor do I wish that this savage War should come to this country and its cities, but I sincerely tell you that I shall not be aggrieved if a few bombs are dropped on the Indian cities. This will open your eyes and you will then understand the issues facing the country.

Nowhere in the world are people more industrious than in China. A little over two years ago when I went to China, I saw the courage and resolution of the people there who were ready to lay down their lives for the sake of their country. Since then they have risen in my estimation. War has been going on in China for about five years. Calamities have been befalling them and their houses have been ruined but they are still fighting bravely. But at the same time they are building up a new China.

Their schools, colleges and universities are no more in existence but they have not given up education. Instead, the war has given the Chinese Government an impetus and a new vision to spread education into the remotest corners of their country. They have moved their educational centres to the interior. They quickly constructed mud huts and fitted them with whatever equipment they could get. This has, incidentally, galvanized them into action in the realm of education. Thus instead of any setback to education the war has given encouragement to education. In this connection we should not forget the educational efforts of the Republican Government of Spain also during the war.

The Japanese war machine has destroyed Chinese cities, their factories, their buildings, their machinery and their economy. The

Japanese blockade is complete. If the Chinese had not revived their cottage industries to fight the import of Japanese manufactures in Chinese villages, China would have been defeated. The revival of cottage industries has saved the Chinese people from the economic slavery of Japan. And this they have done admirably.

When I visited China, there were about 30,000 Chinese industrial cooperatives. There every village has a cooperative society of its own. So intensive and well-organized is the cooperative movement, that even in the Japanese occupied territories, cooperative societies continue to function. In fact, these cooperatives have given a democratic basis to the Chinese economy. In every village democracy is being evolved. Such is the effect of the Japanese bombs on China. Indians should take a lesson from China.

Cottage industries have their own importance in the economic life of a country, and they are rather indispensable in India. The poverty of India cannot be removed without reviving the cottage industries. I remember a talk I had with an agent of Ford's who had supplied a large number of tractors to Russia. The agent said that while Russia could make use of so many tractors, there was hardly any space for even one tractor to stand in some parts of Bengal. India is so thickly populated.

I am in favour of large-scale industry and I am convinced that India can solve her problems of production, distribution and unemployment with the help of big industries. We have very limited capital at our disposal, and it should not be spent in manufacturing articles which can easily be produced in the villages. People fear that owing to unequal distribution of wealth, big machines and large-scale industrialization would lead to unemployment and other troubles. Such a situation arises only when distribution is not equitable. Therefore we have to ensure that wealth is not accumulated in the hands of a few but is distributed equitably.

We have to bear in mind that our large-scale industries do not ruin our cottage industries, because the problems of poverty and unemployment can be solved only by developing cottage industries. We should produce everything needed in India ourselves.

Selected Works of Jawaharlal Nehru, 1979, XII, pp. 545-46. Speech at the All-India Khadi and Industrial Exhibition, Lucknow, 7 December 1941. From Home Dept. Political (Internal) Section 1941, File No 3/48/41, National Archives of India; and also from *National Herald*, 8 December 1941.

CHAPTER 18

THE NEWSPAPERS AND
THE COMMON MAN

I HAVE been caught by this conference at an unfortunate moment. I am so tired and weary, because of incessant travelling and speaking in the countryside during the last ten days, that my mind is benumbed by the overwhelming experience. I have addressed huge gatherings at many places and this experience has been terrifying. I have come in communion with large numbers of people and seen at close quarters the problem of Indian poverty as it exists. I have moved about in the areas where the influence of newspapers is not felt because no newspapers are read except occasionally, and that too, only Hindi and Urdu newspapers. You sometimes forget the fact that what you print in newspapers do not reach the large numbers of people in the country and the reverse fact is also true that you seldom publish anything about these large numbers. You give publicity to the news about cities, about prominent politicians and their speeches. You are much too generous in giving publicity to persons like me. There is really precious little in the newspapers about the masses of India, their economic and social conditions and their poverty.

Rural India is really forgotten and not thought of at all. There are casually some editorial articles on the poverty in India. Even in cities the chief function of news agencies or reporters appears to be to go to half a dozen prominent individuals, get statements from them and send them for publication. It is necessary that you should have trained people who can go to the countryside, to the slums, and study social conditions as big newspapers do in their countries.

I do not say that you wish to ignore the rural areas, but there is nobody to report them. You have one or two news services and a few correspondents scattered about chiefly in big towns. Thus the picture that you draw is not a picture of the whole of India. When one goes to rural areas and sees signs of utter poverty and degradation, one is shocked, and then one realizes that the problems of the day are essentially the problems of these vast masses of human beings and not those about whom you write leading articles.

I have watched the beginning of the conference from a distance. I was much interested in it. I think that the conference is a good and right move and an inevitable development in the life of newspapers in India. Many of the things that you did or decided to do are not to my liking. I think that you sometimes wobbled when a stricter course might have been more befitting to the dignity of the press and the dignity of India. Nevertheless, I realize that you have your own difficulties, and you have them still.

Generally speaking, a newspaper carries weight. It carries weight if it has an individuality and some kind of a crusading spirit. If it has not got these, it merely expresses the views of some individuals which have some effect of course, but not the type of effect which a newspaper ought to have. Perhaps this is also largely due to the fact that newspapers progressively become huge industries—not only individual industries but soon they reach the next stage of development, perhaps an inevitable stage, although an undesirable one. That is, they become big combines starting a chain of newspapers and dictating policies often detrimental to the interests of the country. Because of these big chains, a newspaper loses its individuality and sanctity which every paper so zealously guards. It tries to preserve some vested interest and presents some particular viewpoint only.

I do not know how it is possible to avoid all this. Nevertheless, it does seem to me a dangerous trend and a harmful development, because a newspaper must, whatever its views might be, maintain a certain integrity about the news. It must give all the news, which are worthy of being given, and it must give them without any distortion.

Your conference can do some good by avoiding any distortion or suppression of news. It seems to me far more dangerous to suppress news than to do anything else in a newspaper.

Unfortunately in India you have to face a great deal of suppression of news by the authorities—a deliberate and definite suppression—and a ban on the publicity of big events. But what is almost equally bad is the sense of fear pervading a newspaper office that if you tell the truth you might get into trouble.

The present atmosphere is not suited for the press which seeks the truth or tries to tell the truth. If you have to function properly you have to contend against it, and you might have to contend against it in future also. One result of the suppression of news is that whenever it comes out it appears in a distorted form—either exaggerated or minimized—and becomes difficult to be believed by people. When people tend to believe that what a newspaper says is only a part of the truth and not the whole truth, that paper is bound to fall in the estimation of the public.

One of the most tragic things that happened because of the suppression of news was the way you dealt with the Bengal famine. In the beginning no news about the famine appeared at all in the newspapers. People died by thousands daily, but there was no mention of it. It was a most astonishing thing. Ultimately one newspaper of Calcutta broke through the cordon and then the news gradually came through. It is impossible for any newspaper to function properly or to serve the public if this kind of practice is followed.

In England, America and elsewhere newspapers have vast circulations, but not much direct influence. Sometimes people vote exactly in opposition to what newspapers tell them to do, because they feel that newspapers are not a proper guide. To some extent it is true that a newspaper is influenced by external factors; it may be influenceed by the advertising revenue, or even by political parties. But the lesser it is the better.

Ultimately it does not pay to suppress news, because suppression of news inevitably makes people get a false idea of the situation. Suppression of news does not alter facts and when facts come to be known they upset people. Once an impression is created that news is suppressed, people do not believe even the news that is not suppressed and thus even a true report does not carry much weight. So the first essential for this conference is to insist upon complete freedom of news. The Government on its part should give complete freedom to the press and should not impede the growth of a free, fearless and powerful press.

You have to face this problem. It is inevitable in the existing conditions to have to suffer the continuous interference of governmental authority, the desire of this authority to suppress news. I exhort the editors not to be carried away, in giving true and nothing but true news to the public, by any outside influence or governmental authority.

As a politician I am in continuous difficulty. I speak too often and I am sometimes misreported. I do not know what to do about it. I cannot go on issuing contradictions every time. Almost always I speak in Hindustani and they are translated into English by reporters. The odd thing is that reports of my speeches in Urdu and Hindi newspapers are retranslations of these English translations and therefore they lack originality. Sometimes there are terrible distortions and people often draw my attention to them. I am referring specially to absolute misrepresentations and complete fabrications in certain Urdu and Hindi newspapers from which I have sometimes personally suffered. I urge that such a practice should be stopped.

I do think that it is important that a more efficient system of news service should be organized in India. If transmission of news takes place in Hindustani, as it is done now in English, it will increase the efficiency of the Indian language newspapers tremendously. First of all you will not have to sit down and translate everything into English and then retranslate them into Hindi or Urdu. You will get more or less the original report. It will save time and increase efficiency. After all, you must realize that, important as the English newspapers are in India, and no doubt they will play an important part for a considerable time to come, the future of journalism in India lies with the language newspapers. For this reason especially, there is the need for improving these papers even more than the English newspapers. You have to improve them through such services as I have suggested and through a better type of personnel.

You have been trying to raise the emoluments, allowances, wages and salaries of newspapermen. There is some complaint specially from the language newspapers that the pay scales have not been fixed high enough. With such little experience as I have, I can say that newspapermen are paid badly and in a large number of cases their pay scales are very low.

Personally I think it is always wrong that there should be a big difference between the pay scales of the highest and the lowest employee in any organization. One of the tests of efficiency should be how little is the difference of income between the man at the top and the man at the bottom. All other differences fade away before this big difference of income. When I look at India I try to compare the difference between the Viceroy's salary and allowances and the income of the peasant. This difference gives me some idea of the Indian social system. I am not prepared to accept that any person is a thousand times better than any other person. Whatever the difference might be in the work the difference in the pay scales should be lessened.

I do appeal to you to consider this—the raising of the standard of the journalists not only in regard to payment, but also in regard to their efficiency. The two should really go together and it is difficult to say which comes first.

Large numbers of workers in newspaper offices, especially in language newspaper offices, are not competent. They are inefficient and do not know their job. This is so because they are not given proper wages. It is a vicious circle which you must break and get competent people by paying adequate wages.

I also feel that the news services in India are not well organized. I remember in my boyhood days I was reading *The Pioneer*, published from Allahabad, from the beginning to the end without ever realizing that an Indian lived in India. Now, of course, there is a tremendous difference in the entire presentation of news, but the social scene in India is still not depicted correctly. A great difference exists between the newspapers owned by the Englishmen and those owned by the Indians. I feel that even the latter, as regards the coverage of news, are not rightly balanced. While they devote too much space to national and anti-governmental news they ignore the various social, cultural and economic problems of the masses.

India is fed in respect of foreign news partly by Reuter, which is a news agency, and partly by a few special correspondents and to a slight extent by some American news agencies. Some years ago when I went to Malaya, there was a new world of news opened out before me. In Singapore I found a flood of American agencies. In Chungking there was a variety of news supplied by an American agency and by Reuter, Tass, Habas, etc. There were all kinds of news from which I could pick and choose. In India one particular agency has the monopoly of news which is unfortunate.

I should like news to come from all sources, but above all I should like your conference and the owners of all newspapers present here to think of starting your own foreign news service. Of course, some of you have correspondents abroad. If a foreign news service is started by you it must be absolutely A-one and quite efficient. An Indian foreign news service should pay particular attention to those aspects which are of interest to India, both from the world standpoint and from our national point of view. It would be difficult for one or two newspapers to organize such a big foreign news service. The burden would be considerable. A number of newspapers could combine for the purpose and appoint their agents. I would like these agents to be posted in some of the important world centres like Washington, London, Paris and Moscow. But I would particularly like them to go to places which are not sufficiently covered by other news agencies.

Whatever the future of India, we are going to have trade, cultural and political contacts with countries in Asia and it is quite likely that questions of common defence may also arise. There is also a possibility of some kind of Asiatic federation. So from every point of view it becomes important that you should develop contacts with Asian countries. There can be no difficulty about funds, if a number of newspapers join together it would be convenient to start with 20 or 30 centres. But you should have competent men for this job. So I would request you to consider this suggestion and push it through quickly.

We live in such rapidly changing times that it becomes very important for us to keep in touch with the varying aspects of news in South East Asia, the Middle East and the rest of the world.

The quality of advertisements appearing in some newspapers sometimes pains me. I appeal to the editors that they should exercise a stricter censorship over advertisements so that undesirable advertisements are not accepted. Personally I hope that when there is a popular government it will come down with a heavy hand on such advertisements and prohibit them without giving the press any choice in the matter.

You have to decide what you are running a newspaper for. Is it an industry for profit ? No newspaper can of course be run unless it is sound financially. It can suffer loss for some time, it cannot suffer loss for ever. It must be self-supporting at least. Owing to technical developments the cost of running a newspaper efficiently has become great.

In running a newspaper you should think in terms of the freedom of news and the freedom of man. The freedom of India, of course, comes in inevitably for every Indian. I want you especially to think in terms of the common man in India, because this common man in India, with whom I have been hobnobbing so much for the last ten days, has been neglected very much. I feel a sense of shame that it should be so. We have neglected him continously in our political arguments and squabbles. So I take leave of you with this appeal that you should think about the common man in India.

Selected Works of Jawaharlal Nehru, 1981, XIV, pp. 613-19. Inaugural address at the All India Newspaper Editors' Conference, Allahabad, 16 February 1946. Based on reports from *The Leader,* 17 February and *National Herald,* 17 and 18 February 1946.

CHAPTER 19

THE NEW ASIA OF OUR DREAMS

AS we meet here today, the long past of Asia rises up before us, the troubles of recent years fade away, and a thousand memories revive. But I shall not speak to you of these past ages with their glories and triumphs and failures, nor of more recent times which have oppressed us so much and which still pursue us in some measure. During the past two hundred years we have seen the growth of Western imperialisms and of the reduction of large parts of Asia to colonial or semi-colonial status. Much has happened during these years, but perhaps one of the notable consequences of the European domination of Asia has been the isolation of the countries of Asia from one another: India always had contacts and intercourse with her neighbouring countries in the North-West, the North-East, the East and the South-East. With the coming of British rule in India these contacts were broken off and India was almost completely isolated from the rest of Asia. The old land routes almost ceased to function and our chief window to the outer world looked out on the sea route which led to England. A similar process affected other countries of Asia also. Their economy was bound up with some European imperialism or other; even culturally they looked towards Europe and not to their own friends and neighbours from whom they had derived so much in the past.

Today this isolation is breaking down because of many reasons, political and other. The old imperialisms are fading away. The land routes have revived and air travel suddenly brings us very near to one another. This Conference itself is significant as an expression of that deeper urge of the mind and spirit of Asia which has persisted in spite of the isolationism which grew up during the years of European domination. As that domination goes, the walls that surrounded us fall down and we look at one another again and meet as old friends long parted.

In this Conference and in this work there are no leaders and no followers. All countries of Asia have to meet together on an equal basis in a common task and endeavour. It is fitting that India should play her part in this new phase of Asian development. Apart from the fact that India herself is emerging into freedom and independence, she is the natural centre and focal point of the many forces at work in Asia. Geography is a compelling factor, and geographically she is so situated as to be the meeting-point of Western and Northern and Eastern and South-East Asia. Because of this, the history of India is a long history of her relations with the other countries of Asia. Streams of culture have come to India from the west and the east and been absorbed in India, producing the rich and variegated culture which is India today. At the same time, streams of culture have flowed from India to distant parts of Asia. If you would know India you have to go to Afghanistan and Western Asia, to Central Asia, to China and Japan and to the countries of South-East Asia. There you will find magnificent evidence of the vitality of India's culture which spread out and influenced vast numbers of people.

There came the great cultural stream from Iran to India in remote antiquity. And then that constant intercourse between India and the Far East, notably China. In later years South-East Asia witnessed an amazing efflorescence of Indian art and culture. The mighty stream which started from Arabia and developed as a mixed Irano-Arabic culture poured into India. All these came to us and influenced us, and yet so great was the powerful impress of India's own mind and culture that it could accept them without being itself swept away or overwhelmed. Nevertheless, we all changed in the proccess and in India today all of us are mixed products of these various influences. An Indian, wherever he may go in Asia, feels a sense of kinship with the land he visits and the people he meets.

I do not wish to speak to you of the past, but rather of the present. We meet here not to discuss our past history and contacts, but to forge links for the future. And may I say here that this Conference, and the idea underlying it, is in no way aggressive or against any other continent or country ? Ever since news of this Conference went abroad some people in Europe and America have viewed it with doubt imagining that this was some kind of a Pan-Asian movement directed against Europe or America. We have no designs against anybody; ours is the great design of promoting peace and progress all over the world. Far too long have we of Asia been petitioners in western courts and chancellories. That story must now belong to the past. We propose to stand on our own feet and to cooperate with all others who are prepared to cooperate with us. We do not intend to be the playthings of others.

In this crisis in world history Asia will necessarily play a vital role. The countries of Asia can no longer be used as pawns by others; they are bound to have their own policies in world affairs. Europe and America have contributed very greatly to human progress and for that we must yield them praise and honour, and learn from them the many lessons they have to teach. But the West has also driven us into wars and conflicts without number and even now, the day after a terrible war, there is talk of further wars in the atomic age that is upon us. In this atomic age Asia will have to function effectively in the maintenance of peace. Indeed there can be no peace, unless Asia plays her part. There is today conflict in many countries, and all of us in Asia are full of our own troubles. Nevertheless, the whole spirit and outlook of Asia are peaceful, and the emergence of Asia in world affairs will be a powerful influence for world peace.

Peace can only come when nations are free and also when human beings everywhere have freedom and security and opportunity. Peace and freedom, therefore have to be considered both in their political and economic aspects. The countries of Asia, we must remember, are very backward and the standards of life are appallingly low. These economic problems demand urgent solution or else crisis and disaster may overwhelm us. We have, therefore, to think in terms of the common man and fashion our political, social and economic structure so that the burdens that have crushed him may be removed, and he may have full opportunity for growth.

We have arrived at a stage in human affairs when the ideal of One World and some kind of a World Federation seem to be essential, though there are many dangers and obstacles in the way. We should work for that ideal and not for any grouping which comes in the way of this larger world group. We, therefore, support the United Nations structure which is painfully emerging from its infancy. But in order to have One World, we must also, in

Asia, think of the countries of Asia cooperating together for that larger ideal.

This Conference, in a small measure, represents this bringing together of the countries of Asia. Whatever it may achieve, the mere fact of its taking place is itself of historic significance. Indeed, this occasion is unique in history, for never before has such a gathering met together at any place. So even in meeting we have achieved much and I have no doubt that out of this meeting greater things will come. Whem the history of our present times is written, this event may well stand out as a landmark which divides the past of Asia from the future. And because we are participating in this making of history, something of the greatness of historic events comes to us all.

This Conference will split up into committees and groups to discuss various problems which are of common concern to all of us. We shall not discuss the internal politics of any country, because that is rather beyond the scope of our present meeting. Naturally we are interested in these internal politics, because they act and react on each other, but we may not discuss them at this stage, for if we do so, we may lose ourselves in interminable arguments and complications. We may fail to achieve the purpose for which we have met. I hope that out of this Conference some permanent Asian Institute for the study of common problems and to bring about closer relations will emerge; also perhaps a School of Asian Studies. Further, we might be able to organize an interchange of visits and exchanges of students and professors so that we might get to know each other better. There is much more we can do, but I shall not venture to enumerate all these subjects for it is for you to discuss them and arrive at some decisions.

We seek no narrow nationalism. Nationalism has a place in each country and should be fostered, but it must not be allowed to become aggressive and come in the way of international development. Asia stretches her hand out in friendship to Europe and America as well as to our suffering brethren in Africa. We of Asia have a special responsibility to the people of Africa. We must help them to their rightful place in the human family. The freedom that we envisage is not to be confined to this nation or that or to a particular people, but must spread out over the whole human

race. That universal human freedom also cannot be based on the
supremacy of any particular class. It must be the freedom of the
common man everywhere and full opportunities for him to
develop.

We think today of the great architects of Asian freedom – Sun
Yat-sen, Zaghlul Pasha, the Ataturk Kemal Pasha and others,
whose labours have borne fruit. We think also of that great figure
whose labours and whose inspiration have brought India to the
threshold of her independence— Mahatma Gandhi. We miss him
at this Conference and I yet hope that he may visit us before our
labours end. He is engrossed in the service of the common man in
India, and even this Conference could not drag him away from it.

All over Asia we are passing through trials and tribulations. In
India also you will see conflict and trouble. Let us not be
disheartened by this; this is inevitable in an age of mighty
transition. There are a new vitality and powerful creative impulses
in all the peoples of Asia. The masses are awake and they demand
their heritage. Strong winds are blowing all over Asia. Let us not
be afraid of them, but rather welcome them for only with their
help can we build the new Asia of our dreams. Let us have faith in
these great new forces and the dream which is taking shape. Let
us, above all, have faith in the human spirit which Asia has
symbolized for long ages past.

Selected Works of Jawaharlal Nehru, Second Series, 1984, II, pp. 505-9. Speech
delivered at the plenary session of the Asian Relations Conference, New Delhi, 23
March 1947. First recorded in Asian Relations (Asian Relations Organization, New
Delhi, 1948).

NOTES AND EXERCISES

CHILDHOOD

GLOSSARY

claret : a kind of red wine

petite : applies to a woman who is small-made with a suggestion of neatness

snuggle : get close for warmth, comfort or affection

revelry : merry-making in a noisy manner

squirt : throw out in a sudden forceful stream from a narrow opening

tableau : usually silent depiction of a scene on stage

alums : silken banners or talismans carried during a Mohurrum procession

squabble : petty and noisy quarrel

pony : small horse

TEXTUAL NOTES

Eurasians : people of mixed European and Asian parentage

Arabian Nights : popularly known as 'A Thousand and One Nights , this collection of Arabic tales is of uncertain date and authorship

happenings in 1857 and 1858 : the first Indian revolt against the British was in 1857. As a result British India came under the direct government of the Crown in accordance with Queen Victoria's proclamation in 1858.

Ramayana : or the life of Rama. The oldest of the Sanskrit epics, the *Ramayana* is written by the sage Valmiki. It is supposed to have been composed in about the fifth century B.C.

Mahabharata : or the Great War of the Bharatas. The great epic poem of the Hindus, probably the longest in the world. The reputed author was Krishna-Dwaipayana, the *Vyasa* or the arranger of the Vedas.

the story of Hasan and Husain : also called Al-Hasanan, 'the two Hasans'. They were the sons of the fourth Muslim Caliph, Ali, by his wife Fatima, daughter of Mohammad the Prophet. Husain, the younger brother of Hasan, revolted against the Yazid but was defeated and killed at Karbala (Iraq) in A.D. 680. Husain is the hero of the religious drama performed annually on the anniversary of his death by the Shi'ites of Persia and India.

COMPREHENSION

1. What were the privileges enjoyed solely by the alien rulers in India ?
2. What happened when Nehru saw his father drinking red wine ?
3. What qualities does Nehru admire most in his father ?
4. How does Nehru describe his mother ?
5. How did Nehru learn a good deal about Indian mythology and folklore ?
6. Why did Nehru, as a child, wish that his birthdays would come more frequently ?
7. What, according to Nehru, is vulgar about Indian marriages ? Whom does he hold responsible for it and why ?
8. What does Nehru say about the life of the poor in India ?
9. What, according to Nehru, is considered the inevitable sign of status in the Kashmiri households in the North and why ?
10. What treatment did Nehru receive from the members of his family after his fall from the pony ?

COMPOSITION

1. Give an account of Nehru's childhood.
2. Discuss some of the ideas and characters that deeply impressed Nehru as a child.
3. Briefly narrate some of the memorable incidents of your childhood.

HARROW

GLOSSARY

shirker : one who evades a task or duty
fascinate : to capture and hold interest
aviation : mechanical flying
semitic : of or belonging to any group of people from S.W.Asia chiefly represented now by Jews and Arabs
susceptible : impressionable or easily affected by emotion

TEXTUAL NOTES

Derby day : the day of the great horse-race held annually on Epsom Downs in the Midlands of England; so called from the Derby stakes instituted by the then Earl of Derby in 1780.
Wright Brothers : Wilbur Wright (1867-1912) and Orville Wright (1871-1948) : American airplane inventors, credited with what could be called the first 'mechanical flight' by man. The brothers jointly developed a power-driven heavier-than-air machine on which they made their first successful flight on 17th December, 1903 near Kitty Hawk, North Carolina, USA.

Santos Dumont : Alberto Santos Dumont (1873-1932), the Brazilian avia-tion pioneer who made a balloon ascent in 1897. He constructed the dirigible airship. In 1909, he produced his famous 'demoiselle' or 'grasshopper' monoplane, the forerunner of the modern light plane.

Farman : Henri Farman (1874-1958) French aviator and aircraft construc-tor. In 1909 he set world records in endurance and speed.

Latham : Hubert Latham, a young Anglo-French engineer. In 1909, he set up an altitute record of 10,058 m (33,000 ft.)

Blériot : Louis Bleriot, a lamp manufacturer, who invented the 'aileron' — a small subsidiary plane hinged to the wing edge to achieve lateral stability, superseding the Wrights' system of 'warping'.

Tikka Sahab : crown prince of an Indian province

Jew : a person whose religion is Judaism; member of a Semitic people, some of whom now live in Israel.

Lala Lajpat Rai : Lala Lajpat Rai (1865-1928), popularly known as the 'Punjab Kesari', was a philanthropist, a prolific writer, a social reformer and a staunch nationalist. He was one of the famous trio 'Lal-Bal-Pal', who organized the Extremist Party and demanded Swaraj.

Tilak : Bal Gangadhar Tilak (1857-1920), popularly known as 'Lokmanya'. He popularized the cult of patriotism. Tilak was also the founder of two newspapers, *The Maratha* in English and *Kesari* in Marathi. He declared, 'Swaraj is my birthright and I shall have it'. He preached the political ideals of self-help and national revival among the masses. He tried to create a strong national feeling among the Indian people by reminding them of their heroic past.

G.M.Trevelyan : George Macaulay Trevelyan (1876-1962), English historian, known for his defence and illustration of history as a literary art.

Garibaldi : Guiseppe Garibaldi, (1807-1882), Italian patriot and soldier who was the key military figure in the creation of the united kingdom of Italy.

COMPREHENSION

1. How did Nehru feel when left to himself amongst strangers in England ?
2. What did Nehru think of most English boys and how did he find himself vis-a-vis them ?
3. How did Nehru surprise his form master ?
4. What subjects, besides politics, fascinated Nehru most ?
5. Who was the Indian boy at Harrow and why did Nehru find him a misfit ?
6. What prompted the-house-master to pay a sudden nocturnal visit to the pupils' rooms ?

7. What was the news from India that greatly agitated Nehru ?
8. How did Nehru feel when he finished reading the Garibaldi books ?
9. What did Nehru feel on the eve of his departure from Harrow ?

COMPOSITION

1. Give an account of Nehru's life at Harrow.
2. Write a note on the last two years of your life at school.

AN ADVENTURE IN THE HIMALAYAS

GLOSSARY

plateau : a large, relatively flat land area raised above adjacent land on at
   least one side
verdant : green with growing plants
glacier : a large body of ice moving very slowly down a mountain slope
   or valley
diadem : a crown or a head-band showing royalty
amphitheatre : a round or oval building with rows of seats one above
   another, ranged about an arena and used in ancient Rome for public
   shows. Also a flat or gently sloping area surrounded by abrupt slopes.
crevasse : a deep crack, especially applied to a cleft in a glacier or the
   earth
fissure : narrow opening or crack of considerable length and depth

TEXTUAL NOTES

the cave of Amaranath : believed to be the abode of Lord Shiva; hence, a
   place of pilgrimage for the Hindus
geological age : a distinct period (with common geological features)
   in the evolution of the physical history of the earth. (Geology—a
   science that deals with the history, composition, structure and
   changes of the earth as recorded in rocks.)
Manasarovar : situated to the south of the Kailas range of mountains,
   generally recognized as the highest body of fresh water in the world.
   The lake has crystal clear, turquoise water. A holy place for Hindus.
Kailas : elevation 22,027 ft. It is one of the highest mountain ranges in
   western Tibet. Known to the Hindus as Shiva's abode ; it is a place of
   pilgrimage for both the Hindus and the Buddhists. The latter call it
   Mount Meru.
Walter de la Mare : British poet (1873-1956)

COMPREHENSION

1. What did Nehru see from the top of the Zoji-la pass ? Try and
   describe what he felt.

2. How did Nehru find his journey across the glaciers ?
3. What happened when Nehru stepped into fresh snow ?
4. What resolve did Nehru make after his adventure in the Himalayas and why ?
5. Was the resolve fulfilled ? Give reasons for your answer.
6. Briefly explain the meaning of the stanza of the poem Nehru has quoted at the end of the chapter.

COMPOSITION

1. Briefly narrate Nehru's experience during his visit to the Himalayas.
2. Why was the journey across the Himalayas a challenge to Nehru ? Why would Nehru believe that such journeys are worth the making ?
3. Relate any exciting journey or adventure that you had while at school.

ANIMALS IN PRISON

GLOSSARY

rafter : sloping beam supporting a roof
imperturbability : the mental state of calm; the quality of not being touched by agitation
gaunt : of a pinched appearance; thin and grim
glisten : shine somewhat dully
habitation : dwelling or residence
eerie : weird; arousing fear
stalk : to approach or pursue without being noticed
uncouth : ungraceful; grotesque

TEXTUAL NOTES

Pavlov's reflex : a reaction produced automatically in response to stimulus, a discovery made by Ivan Petrovich Pavlov (1849-1936), the Russian physiologist and experimental psychologist. Pavlov's pioneering work on digestion won him a Nobel prize.

COMPREHENSION

1. How did Nehru view the regular walks outside the lock-up ?
2. What did the sight of the Himalayas mean to Nehru during his prison days ?
3. How did Nehru feel in his cell when the monsoon rains came pouring down in Dehra Dun ?
4. What did Nehru observe about the behaviour of squirrels ?
5. How did the mynahs become Nehru's pets in jail ?

6. When and how did Nehru realize the appropriateness of the name given to the Brain-Fever bird ?
7. How was the little monkey rescued by its parents ? Why did Nehru find this incident impressive ?
8. How did the convict overseers enjoy greater freedom than ordinary prisoners ?
9. What does Nehru say about the effect of pets upon long-term convicts in jail ?
10. How did Nehru find himself nursing the puppy ?
11. What does Nehru think of the general Indian attitude towards keeping animals as pets ?
12. What does Nehru find so incongruous about the attitude of Hindus towards the cow ?
13. What makes Nehru think that patron animals have greatly shaped the national character of different countries ?
14. How does Nehru explain the mild temper and non-violent character of the Hindus ?

COMPOSITION

1. Describe Nehru's life in different jails.
2. How does Nehru view his strange companionship with the animals during his life in the jails ? Elucidate, with specific references to the lesson.
3. Write a note on the bird or animal you like the most.

LIFE'S PHILOSOPHY

GLOSSARY

symposium : a collection of opinions on a subject; especially one published by a periodical
superstition : deep-rooted but unfounded general belief or practice
dogmatic : pertaining to a dogma or stating an opinion in a very positive or arrogant manner as if expressing established fact
credulousness : to believe easily without sufficient evidence
supernatural : miraculous; above or beyond visible nature
bigoted : intolerantly and blindly devoted to a belief or opinion
tentative : not fully worked out or developed, hesitant
psychical : having extraordinary or mysterious sensitivity, perception or understanding
mysticism : belief and teaching that knowledge of God and of real truth may be obtained through meditation or spiritual insight, independent of the mind and the sense
metaphysics : the science which investigates the first principles of nature and thought; abstract or philosophical

flabby : yielding; lacking firmness; feeble

premise : presupposition; a statement in logic based on which conclusions are drawn

dabble : to do anything in a trifling or small way

spiritualism : the doctrine that the spirit has a real existence apart from matter

seánce : a meeting at which spiritualists try to communicate with the dead

deity : a god or goddess

anthropomorphic : representation of a god as having the form, personality or attributes of man

monism : a philosophical theory that a complex entity (such as the universe) is basically simple and undifferentiated

incursion : sudden attack or invasion

pagan : a heathen; a follower of a religion having many gods

pantheistic : pertaining to the belief that all forces and laws of nature are God

smother : stifle; suppress

riddle : a puzzling question; a mystifying problem or fact

creed : a set of fundamental beliefs

collocation : placing together; arrangement

corollary : easy inference; supplement

TEXTUAL NOTES

atma : (also known as atman) the soul; the principle of life

the Karma theory : the Hindu and Buddhist theory that a person's actions decide his destiny in the next existence

Advaita : without a second. (All is resolved into a single God who is 'Advaita.')

Vedanta : the end or object of the Vedas (lit.Sanskrit). Classical system of Indian philosophy which refers to the teaching of the Upanishads (the last section of the Vedas) and also to the knowledge of its ultimate meaning.

non-duality of mind and matter : a metaphysical view that mind and matter are not two distinct substances but only two aspects of the same substance

dialectic of continuous change : the logical disputation that the essence of reality is change

original sin : the tendency towards sinfulness believed, by all Christians, to be inherent in mankind as a result of Adam's disobedience

fascism : extreme right-wing totalitarian political system or views which originally prevailed in Italy under Mussolini (1922-1943)

nazism : The political system of the German National Socialist Party laid down by Adolf Hitler in the Third Reich. It combines an appeal to extreme and exclusive nationalism with the predominance of groups assumed to be racially superior.

Socialist theory : Political and economic theory of social organisation advocating state ownership and control of natural resources and commercial activities. The main characteristics of the theory are: the equal natural right of all men to the enjoyment of the goods provided by nature; the universal obligation to labour, the universal right to education and the necessity of abolishing both riches and poverty in the interests of human happiness.

Space-time : The development of Einstein's theory of Relativity has led to the disappearance of a clear-cut distinction between three dimensional space and an independent time. In the modern view space and time are considered as being welded together in a four dimensional space-time continuum.

Quantum Theory : The theory that grew up around Max Planck's introduction to Physics of the concept of the discontinuity of energy. It establishes that energy and some other physical properties often exist in tiny, distinct amounts. The theory has helped man to understand the secrets of the atomic and sub- atomic world.

Bertrand Russell : (1872-1970); the British mathematician, philosopher and social reformer who made original and decisive contributions to logic and mathematics and wrote with distinction in all fields of philosopy.

COMPREHENSION

1. What does Nehru say happened to his ideas and ideals held in his youth ?
2. What does Nehru say about the essence of human nature and why ?
3. What does Nehru think of the relationship between ends and means ?
4. What was the basis of Nehru's approach to life in his early years ?
5. What does Nehru think of religion in its practised form ? And why are most people in the world attracted to religion ?
6. What are the areas of life that Nehru feels belong to science ? And what does he call the limitations of science vis-a-vis human life ?
7. Why does mysticism irritate Nehru ?
8. Briefly state Nehru's personal experience in following the lines of metaphysical thought ?
9. Where does Nehru say his chief interests lie ?
10. How is Nehru disposed towards the *Karma* theory ?
11. How does Nehru view the question of spiritualism ?
12. What approach does Nehru prescribe for understanding the mysteries of the world ?

13. What is Nehru's attitude towards the popular idea of a personal God ?
14. What does Nehru think of the *Vedanta* ?
15. What is Nehru's reaction to the world of nature around him ?
16. How has Gandhi's thinking influenced Nehru's philosophy of life ?
17. In what way did the study of Marx and Lenin influence Nehru? And what were Nehru's views on the Soviet Revolution ?
18. Why does Nehru consider individual freedom both important and essential ? How does one achieve it ?
19. What has Nehru to say about the advancement of human knowledge and the need for it ?
20. Why do human beings take refuge in irrational social prejudices ?
21. What does Nehru think are the problems involved in removing social evils ? How does he think these problems can be tackled ?
22. What, according to Nehru, are the limitations of scientific and rational thinking ?
23. Why does Nehru find the Communist approach to world issues inadequate ?
24. How does Nehru define the problems of the individual and what are his solutions to them ?
25. How does Nehru find intuition useful in life ?
26. What does Nehru mean by a 'living philosophy' ?
27. How does Nehru compare the modern generation with the medieval ?
28. How do the developments in physics help Nehru see a fundamental unity in nature ?
29. What does Nehru find common between the *Advaita Vedantic* theory and some of the conclusions of modern science ?
30. How does Nehru find science substantially enriching the contents of human life ?
31. How does Nehru find science and philosophy different from each other in their purposes ?
32. What does Nehru fear the most about science and why ?
33. What does Nehru mean by the 'internal conflict of the spirit of man' ? Where does he perceive its workings ?
34. How does Nehru visualize the future of man ?

COMPOSITION

1. Why does Nehru advocate a scientific approach to life in preference to a religious one ? Discuss.
2. What makes Nehru believe that all doctrines are limited in their application to life? What does Nehru suggest as an alternative ?
3. Write a note on Nehru as a champion of personal freedom.

GROWTH AND DECAY

GLOSSARY

millennium : a thousand years
confederacy : a league or alliance of confederate states
barbarous : uncivilized, brutal, harsh
renascence : (also renaissance) being born anew, a period of vigorous
   artistic and intellectual activity
lexicographer : one who compiles or edits a dictionary
fable : fictitious tale
legend : marvellous traditional story (true or invented) handed down
   from the past
hallmark : mark of authenticity or good quality
secular : independent of religion
dialectician : a logician, skilled at discourse
sterile : unfruitful; barren
rejuvenate : restore to youthful condition
mumble : speak indistinctly in a subdued voice
impoverish : make poor
peasantry : usually poor people who farm the soil
serf : slave
regressive : going back or declining
tenacity : toughness; persistence; holding fast

TEXTUAL NOTES

Christian era : the period (in Christian countries) since the (assumed)
   year of Jesus' birth
Gupta Empire : Indian dynasty ruling from A.D. 320 to A.D. 550
the White Huns : a race of fierce barbarians who came from the steppes
   of north-central Asia. In the fifth century A.D. the Huns spread in
   devastating hordes over some of the fairest provinces of the Roman
   Empire in the West and the Gupta Empire in India.
the last of the great Guptas : Skanda Gupta (A.D. 455 to A.D. 467)
Yashovarman : probably belonged to an old family known as Aulikara
   whose members ruled Malwa since the fourth century A.D.
Indo-Aryan races : the branch of Aryans who came to India around 1500
   B.C.
Harsha : One of north India's most celebrated heroes, Harsha was a
   gifted warrior, a great administrator, and a sensitive poet and
   playwright. He was also a generous patron of religions and the arts.
   Harsha was the ruler of Kanauj from A.D. 606 to A.D. 647.
Mihira Bhoja : He was king of Kanauj in the 9th century A.D. and

belonged to the imperial dynasty of the Pratiharas.

Rajashekhara : the court-poet of the Pratihara king Mahendrapala (9th century A.D.)

Indian colonies : These existed in South-East Asian countries such as Indonesia, Malaysia and modern Kampuchea in the Far East.

Shankara : the Indian philosopher and reformer who founded the *Advaita* or the non-dualist school of *Vedanta* philosophy. He is believed to have lived in the eighth-ninth century A.D.

Tantric worship : in Hinduism and Buddhism. It is known for the use of *mantra*(mystical words); *mandala* (sacred diagrams); worship of *Shakti* (female deities); and ritual use of wine, meat, and sexual intercourse, in order to awaken the force called *Kundalini* and merge with the Godhead.

Yoga system : Literally 'yoga' means 'harnessing' or 'yoking' of one's faculties. The 'yoga system' refers to a certain range of methods of contemplation used in the Indian religious tradition both Hindu and non-Hindu; it also refers to a recognized school of Hindu metaphysics allied to a particular contemplative technique.

Bhavabhuti : an illustrious poet patronized by Yashovarman, king of Kanauj, in the early half of the eighth century A.D.

Bhaskara II : a celebrated mathematician and astronomer who was born early in the eleventh century A.D. It has been claimed for Bhaskara that he was fully acquainted with the principles of Differential Calculus.

Gothic art : pertaining mainly to a style of architecture originating in France in the middle of the 12th century and existing in the western half of Europe till the middle of the 16th century. It is characterized by the use of the pointed arch and the ribbed vault, fine woodwork and stonework and by a progressive lightening of structure.

the Cholas : A.D. 900-1267. The Cholas rose to importance during this period and occupied the present Tanjore and Trichinapalli districts in the far south of India, beyond the Venkata Hills.

Sri Vijaya : a small kingdom in the Malay peninsula that was conquered by Rajendra Chola Deva I around A.D. 1021.

Radhakrishnan : Sarvapalli Radhakrishnan (1888-1975), the Indian philosopher-statesman who was a very articulate interpreter of the Hindu tradition, and independent India's second President.

Sylvain Lévi : French Indologist

'La culture... pedantesque.' : 'With the loss of its liberty India has also lost its Sanskrit culture. New languages, new literatures have invaded Aryan territory and Sanskrit is like a poor refugee in colleges, and it has taken on a pedantic air.'

'Mais... insu.' : Though Indian eyes follow the word of the ancients, their intelligence reveal new ideas. India has transformed itself

without knowing it.
the fall of Rome : in the fifth century A.D.
the Roman Empire : 27 B.C. to A.D. 284
Kshatriya : the warrior-class and, sometimes, the ruling class

COMPREHENSION

1. What does Nehru say India was like during the first one thousand years of the Christian era ?
2. What did Nehru discover in the literature of the classical Age of India ?
3. What, as told by Nehru, was the effect of the Hun invasion upon the Indo-Aryan race ?
4. What was the condition of India, according to Nehru, during the rule of Harsha ?
5. What does Nehru tell us about Bhoja of the eleventh century ?
6. How did South India become more important than North India ? · And what reasons does Nehru give for this change ?
7. What was the importance of Benares in the North ?
8. Why was Nalanda an important university and what was Nalanda's contribution to the spread of Indian culture abroad ?
9. How does Nehru describe the Indian philosophers after Shankara ?
10. During what period of Indian history was Indian art at its peak and why ?
11. When did India suffer a cultural stagnation and why ?
12. Why did the Roman Empire collapse ?
13. What happened to the Indians who had ventured out in search of opportunities abroad ?
14. What led to the rise of the spirit of exclusiveness in India and what was the consequence ?
15. In what way did Nehru find the Indian social structure providing stability to her civilization ?
16. When did the social structure in India become regressive and what was the general effect of the regression upon the Indian civilization?

COMPOSITION

1. Briefly outline the social changes in India under the Guptas and analyze the factors responsible for such changes.
2. Write a note on the factors responsible for the decline of the Indian civilization as stated by Nehru.

DEVELOPMENT OF A COMMON CULTURE

GLOSSARY

edifice : a large structure or organization

petrifaction : making lifeless or inactive; deadening

monotheism : the belief in only one God

tenuous :   thin, slender, here rarefied

proselytization : conversion from one faith to another

census : official counting of population

seclusion : isolation; screened or hidden from view

chastity : virginity, sexual purity

gentry : an upper class of people though not of the nobility

cue : signal; hint

chivalry : the qualities or code of an ideal gentleman, such as courage, integrity and consideration for women and the weak

mythology : a body of myths especially those dealing with gods, demigods and legendary heroes of a particular people, usually involving supernatural elements

theological : pertaining to the study of God through a religious system or theory

medieval : belonging to the Middle Ages; old-fashioned

static : unchanging; stationary

swerve : deviate

feeble : weak, lacking in energy or strength, in character or intelligence; ineffective

TEXTUAL NOTES

Akbar : Akbar (1542-1605) was the third Moghul emperor of India. He came to power in 1556.

Vaishnavite : one belonging to the Vaishnav sect, which worships Vishnu as the Supreme Deity

Tulsidas : (1532-1623) The greatest and the most famous of the Hindi poets, Tulsidas is widely known for his *Rama-Charita-Manas*.

Rana Pratap : (1572-1597) son of Udai Singh of Mewar, a great Rajput warrior

COMPREHENSION

1. How did Indian art change itself under the Moghul rule and become different ?
2. What, according to Nehru, kept the Moghul rulers strong ?
3. What does Nehru consider to be Aurungzeb's contribution to the downfall of the Moghul Empire ?
4. What were the effects of the Islamic invasion of India ? Why did Islam appeal to some in the Hindu fold ?
5. Why does Nehru feel that Islam did not hold any appeal for the upper-caste Hindus ?
6. Why, according to Nehru, did most conversions take place in

groups ?

7. In which occupations, in modern India, does Nehru see signs of mass conversions to Islam having taken place in the past ?

8. What was the status of the women in India during the Moghul period ?

9. What is Nehru's view about the portrayal of women in the Hindi *Rama-Charita-Manas* by Tulsidas ?

10. What were the common traits between the Hindus and the Muslims and how did they develop ?

11. What was the effect of the *purdah* system upon society in general ?

12. How did the Hindu and Muslim communities interact in the villages of India ?

13. To which community did most of the traders belong and how did they interact with the others ?

14. Who was Khankhana and what did he say about Rana Pratap ?

15. What did Akbar like best about the Rajputs and what was his attitude towards them ?

16. In what way did Akbar contribute to keep the reigns of his successors free from trouble ?

COMPOSITION

1. Write a note on the growth of a common culture in Indian society during the Moghul period.

2. Briefly discuss how a common culture between people belonging to various faiths would contribute to a stronger sense of national unity in present-day India.

AND THEN GANDHI CAME

GLOSSARY

Extremist : person recommending extreme political measures

Moderate : person avoiding extreme political measures; holder of temperate and reasonable views

hovel : small or wretched dwelling

inexorable : unrelenting

derelict : forsaken; abandoned; decaying

beacon-light : a source of inspiration

déclassé : fallen or lowered in class or social position

morass : marsh; something that confuses or impedes

bourgeoisie : the middle class, mainly tradespeople and white-collar workers

tenacious : stubborn

murky : dark, gloomy and obscure

quagmire : wet, boggy ground, a situation that threatens to become inextricable

fell disease : deadly; (here) tuberculosis

quack : charlatan; a pretender to knowledge and skill that he does not possess, especially in the world of medicine

incessant : continual, without stopping

appalling : horrifying

TEXTUAL NOTES

World War I : (1914-1918) the war between Austria, Germany, Bulgaria, Turkey etc. on the one hand and England, France, the USSR, the USA on the other. It ended with the defeat of Germany.

Moslem League : Formally inaugurated on December 30, 1906 the Moslem League was a body established to look after the political rights and interests of the Muslim community in the Indian subcontinent.

British Trade Union Congress : Trade unions are associations of workers for the purpose of improving their economic status and working conditions through collective bargaining. The first trade unions came about in Great Britain in the nineteenth century.

Martial Law : Martial Law was imposed on Punjab from 15 April to 25 August 1919 following the Jallianwala Bagh massacre.

Tagore : Rabindranath Tagore (1861-1941), the Bengali poet and philosopher, who was awarded the Nobel prize in Literature in 1913, for his book of poems, *Gitanjali*.

Janaka : The king of Videha and father of Sita in the *Ramayana*. Janaka was famed for his wisdom, his great knowledge and his innate goodness.

Yajnavalka : The celebrated sage to whom are attributed works like *Shukla* or the 'White' *Yajur-Veda* and the *Satapatha Brahmana*. According to the latter work, he flourished in the court of Janaka.

Alcibiades : (450 B.C. to 404 B.C.) Athenian general and statesman.

a Corybant : one of the Corybantes who were worshippers of goddess Cybele of Phrygia (who represented the fecundity of nature). It is known that the Corybantes had a mystic cult and that a prominent feature of their ritual was a wild dance.

Pericles : (495-429 B.C.) Pericles was the leading statesman of Athens for an unusually long period. He took Athens to the height of its political power and artistic achievement. The years from 446 B.C. to 429 B.C. have been called the Periclean Age.

Maryas : a legendary Greek youth who boasted of being more musical than Apollo and challenged the god to a contest.

Socrates : (469 B.C. to 399 B.C.) the Greek philosopher and logician, Socrates was an important formative influence on Plato and had a profound effect on ancient philosophy.

COMPREHENSION

1. How did Nehru read the political scene in India during World War I ?
2. Why was Nehru shocked to see the life of the industrial workers in India during the first World War ?
3. How does Nehru describe the life of the labourers in the Assam tea gardens ?
4. Why does Nehru think that India was a derelict nation at the end of World War I ?
5. Why does Nehru feel pity for the intellectuals in India at the end of the War ?
6. Whom does Nehru call the 'petty bourgeoisie' and how did they fare in India in the postwar era ?
7. How does Nehru say the conditions were ripe in India for Gandhi to come ?
8. What, according to Nehru, is the essence of Gandhi's teachings ?
9. What, according to the ancient books, is the function of a leader ?
10. Against whom and what did Gandhi raise his voice ?
11. What does one do to overcome fear ?
12. How did Gandhi, as told by Nehru, bring about a transformation in the Indian character ?
13. What was the popular reaction to Gandhi and his teachings ?
14. What does Nehru say about Gandhi's ideal of truth ?
15. How do Alcibiades' words on a great orator apply to Gandhi ?

COMPOSITION

1. Write a note, after Nehru, on the condition of Indian society before Gandhi came upon the scene, and discuss Gandhi's influence upon the masses.
2. What was the essence of Gandhi's teachings ?
3. Do you think Gandhi has had any influence on the present generation in India ? State your reasons for saying yes or no.

TRYST WITH DESTINY

GLOSSARY

tryst : an appointment to meet
redeem : fulfil
quest : search
grandeur : the quality of being large and impressive
sovereign : supreme in power and authority
homage : mark or testimony (by word or action) of esteem

TEXTUAL NOTES

the greatest man of our generation : Gandhi

the Appointed Day : 15 August 1947
the Father of our nation :Gandhi
Jai Hind : victory to India; a form of salutation to the motherland, popularized by Netaji

COMPREHENSION

1. When did Nehru deliver the speech *Tryst with Destiny* ? How was it a rare moment in history ?
2. What did Nehru expect the Assembly to do ?
3. What did India struggle for? What, according to Nehru, was the source of India's strength during her struggle ?
4. What did Nehru consider as the sorrows of the past and how did he visualize the 'challenge of the future' ?
5. How did Nehru intend to serve India ?
6. Whom did Nehru consider 'the greatest man of our generation' and what was his ambition ?
7. What was Nehru's idea of the One World ?
8. What appeal did Nehru make on behalf of the Assembly to the people of India in his address ?
9. In what way did Nehru find the 'Appointed Day' significant ?
10. How did the political boundary cut off some people from us ? What was Nehru's message for them ?
11. What role did Nehru envisage for the people of India to play in shaping their future ?

COMPOSITION

1. 'Nehru was a man of vision'. Elaborate the statement with reference to *Tryst with Destiny*.
2. Briefly state how you wish to serve your country in the future.
3. Discuss the evils of communalism in present-day India.

THE CULTIVATION OF A SCIENTIFIC OUTLOOK

GLOSSARY

manifestation : the act of making clear; form
imperialism : the making of empires; the gaining of political and trade advantages over a poorer nation
immoral : violating standards of moral behaviour
axiom : self-evident truth, universally accepted
composite : made up of various parts which are complete in themselves
connotation : the implication of a word, apart from its primary meaning

TEXTUAL NOTES

The Wardha Scheme of Education : Scheme prepared by a committee that met at Wardha in 1937 with Dr. Zakir Hussain as the chairman. It recommended that physical work should go hand in hand with intellectual training. This system of education is also known as 'Basic Education'.

Newton's theory of Gravitation : Gravitation is a force of mutual attraction between all bodies, of which the falling of bodies to earth is one instance. The theoretical understanding of this phenomenon was given by Sir Isaac Newton (A.D. 1642-1727).

Einstein's theory : The theory of Relativity formulated by Albert Einstein, the German physicist who settled in the U.S.A. It recognizes the impossibility of determining absolute motion and leads to the concept of a four dimensional space-time continuum.

the League of Nations : association of self-governing States formed in Paris in 1919 after World War I in order to promote international cooperation and to achieve international peace and security. Unable to stop aggression by major powers it collapsed during World War II. In 1945 it was superseded by the United Nations.

COMPREHENSION

1. Why does Nehru condemn the educational system as it existed then in India ?
2. What kind of educational system does Nehru want for India ?
3. What, does Nehru say, would happen t society when individuals are highly developed ?
4. How, according to Nehru, does the social structure condition the development of the individual ?
5. How does Nehru assess the international environment of his time and its effect upon the people of the world ?
6. What was the cause of intellectual paralysis all over the world in Nehru's time ?
7. What forms of government does Nehru mention, and how does every form of government maintain itself ?
8. What does Nehru say about the men privileged to enjoy freedom of thought ?
9. State the drawback of the democratic process, as stated by Nehru.
10. Why does Nehru consider the period after 1914 as a time of transition and how long does he think it will last ?
11. What are Nehru's views on how India's composite culture came about ?
12. How have alien and invading cultures been received in India ?
13. How does Nehru describe the new culture from the West ? What was its basis ?
14. How did Western culture come to India ? How was it received by the Indians ?

15. How does Nehru distinguish 'science' from political conquest ?
16. How does Nehru define science ? What does science teach mankind ?
17. In which areas does Nehru want the people to adopt the methods of science ?
18. What irrational elements does Nehru find in our social and economic systems ?
-19. What are Nehru's allegations against some of the members of the League of Nations ?
20. Why does the socialist approach to the world's problems appeal to Nehru ?
21. What, according to Nehru, is the real joy of life and how does one attain it ?

COMPOSITION

1. Write a note on Nehru's ideas about science.
2. How does Nehru define culture ? Discuss Nehru's various approaches to the problems inherent in Indian culture during his time.
3. What do you have to say about Nehru's claim of his being a socialist ? Cite examples from the piece you have studied supporting your views.

THE GOOD AND BAD APPLICATIONS OF SCIENCE

GLOSSARY

grappling with : seizing and struggling with
oligarchy : government or rule by a few, (often) for their own interests
cavalry man : soldier who fights on horseback
smouldering : burning slowly without a flame (fire lingering in a suppressed state)

TEXTUAL NOTES

Industrial Revolution : In the popular sense, this term is regarded as being synonymous with the development of spinning and weaving machines, James Watt's steam engine, the railway locomotive and the factory system. The term was first popularized by the English economic historian Arnold Toynbee (1852-1883) to describe England's economic development from 1760-1840. In fact, a series of fundamental, technological, economic, social and cultural changes taken together constitute the Industrial Revolution.
capitalistic system : Economic system by which ownership of capital or wealth, the production and distribution of goods, and the reward of labour are entrusted to, and effected by, private enterprise.

great depression : Depression is a term used in Economics to denote a major downswing in the business cycle. A depression is characterized by sharply reduced industrial production, widespread unemployment and a general contraction of business activity. The depression that began in 1929 was the most severe and widespread economic decline in the first half of the twentieth century.

French Revolution : (1789-1794) The corrupt Bourbon kings were ousted and France was declared a Republic. The Revolution came to an end when Napoleon took all powers into his own hands. The French Revolution gave us the modern ideas of democracy, nationalism and equality.

Russian Revolution : The revolution in 1917 resulted in the overthrow of Russian serf dom and the emergence of the Socialist State.

COMPREHENSION

1. What does Nehru consider to be the challenge of the human mind ?
2. How has science, according to Nehru, made modern life different from that of the past ?
3. How, does Nehru believe, will the world's population survive in the future ?
4. What has Nehru to say in favour of the improved machines ?
5. How does Nehru see the life of the people change as machines steadily displace workers in factories ?
6. Why was Nehru so confident in predicting the failure of intense nationalism in various countries of the world ? How did he visualize its consequences ?
7. Why does Nehru prefer peaceful mass action to violent uprisings as a means of achieving freedom ?
8. How does Nehru visualize the horrors of a new world war and anticipate the end of civilization ?
9. What does Nehru mean by 'Fear has big eyes' ?
10. What, according to Nehru, are the two processes going on in the world ?

COMPOSITION

1. Discuss after Nehru, the good and bad applications of science in the modern world.
2. What makes Nehru fear that science would one day bring about universal destruction to human civilization ? Give examples.
3. Write a note on the application of science in the daily life of the people today.

WOMEN AND THE FREEDOM MOVEMENT

GLOSSARY

womanish : effeminate

drag : draw with effort or difficulty
emancipation : the act of setting free from bondage
adrift : cut loose
coterie : an exclusive group of people

TEXTUAL NOTES

Harijans : Members of certain Indian castes, though Hindus, were excluded from the ordinary social and religious privileges of Hinduism. Gandhiji called these underprivileged people the 'Harijans' or 'the children of God'

Sita : Janaka's daughter and the loyal devoted wife of Rama in the *Ramayana*. In the *Vedas* however, Sita was a furrow or husbandry personified and worshipped as a deity presiding over agriculture and fruit.

Savitri : Daughter of king Aswapati and beloved of Satyavan whom she insisted on marrying although she was warned by a seer that he had only one year left to live. Savitri's devotion to her husband pleased Yama, the god of Death, and he was finally constrained to restore the dead Satyavan to life.

Civil Disobedience Movement : (1930-1934) The Lahore Session of the Congress on December 31, 1929 authorized the All India Congress Committee to launch the Civil Disobedience Movement to attain the goal of 'Purna Swaraj' (complete independence).

COMPREHENSION

1. How does one judge the advancement of a nation ?
2. What, does Nehru say, Indian men should do to make the nation progressive ?
3. How does Nehru define the depressed classes ? Why does he think that all of us belong to them ?
4. What does Nehru advise the women to do to ensure their position in public life in the future ?
5. What did the women in the north do in 1930 which raised them in the estimation of the world ?
6. What does Nehru say is the fundamental question facing the world ?
7. What does Nehru suggest the Indian women to do about their responsibilities ?
8. What, according to Nehru, was the common urge of people at the time ? How did Nehru want the women, in particular, to function ?

COMPOSITION

1. Bring out Nehru's ideas on the role of women in public life as stated in *Women and the Freedom Movement*.
2. How does Nehru visualize the emancipation of women in India ?

What does he expect the women to do in order to achieve this end ?
3. Give your own suggestions for the upliftment of women in present-day Indian society.

THE LITERATURES OF INDIA

GLOSSARY

queer : strange; dubious
provincialism : being limited in outlook, narrow-minded
fountainhead : source; beginning
dialect : anything transmitted from ancestors or past ages; a legacy
colloquial : pertaining to common or informal conversation
orthodox : conforming to established doctrine
ballad : a simple and straightforward narrative poem in short stanzas
regimentation : excessive or strict control

TEXTUAL NOTES

P.E.N. : the club, an international association for Poets, Playwrights, Essayists, Editors and Novelists.
Sir Mirza : Sir Mirza Ismail, former (pre-Independence) Prime Minister of Travancore and Cochin

COMPREHENSION

1. How does Nehru define his place in the P.E.N. as a writer ?
2. What does Nehru have to say about the 'language problem' of the time ?
3. What does Nehru think of the Sanskrit language ? Why does he say that Sanskrit had a restraining influence and was also a unifying force ?
4. In what way were the Indian languages affected by Persian ? How did Persian become a part of the Indian national heritage ?
5. What does Nehru find common between Urdu and Hindi ? What has Nehru to say regarding the growth of the literary forms in both these languages ?
6. What does Nehru say about the future of the literary devices in both Urdu and Hindi and why ?
7. Why does Nehru believe that language reflects the life of the people ?
8. What does Nehru find happening in the lives of the people when there is a divorce between the language of the learned class and that of the masses ?
9. What is the contribution of the provincial languages to our national identity, as seen by Nehru ?
10. Why does Nehru consider the mutual dependence of the Indian

languages essential for their growth ?

11. Do politics affect languages ? Or are languages themselves a destructive factor ? Give Nehru's views on this with regard to the political developments on the Indian subcontinent.

12. What does Nehru think are the pre-conditions for the growth of literature ?

13. Why does Nehru rebel against the idea of authority ?

14. Why does Nehru consider political freedom an essential one ?

COMPOSITION

1. Bring out Nehru's ideas about the provincial literatures of India and their contributions to a greater national identity.

2. Write a note, after Nehru, on the influence of Sanskrit and Persian on the provincial languages of India.

3. Write a note on the national language policy in modern India.

SOME FAMOUS WRITERS

GLOSSARY

abstruse : hidden; difficult to understand

autocracy : government in which one person has unlimited power; despotism

conservatism : stability, preferring gradual development to abrupt change

reactionary : one who is opposed to change

tussle : a sharp struggle

blight : to have a deteriorating or destructive effect

exemplar : a person or a thing worth imitating; the ideal model·

TEXTUAL NOTES

Voilá un homme ! : What a man !

Commune of Paris : insurrectionary government formed in Paris (1792) during the French Revolution. It played a leading part in the Reign of Terror until suppressed in 1794, when the Moderates gained control of the National Convention in France.

COMPREHENSION

1. Why does Nehru believe that the study of art and literature would prove to be a rewarding experience ?

2. What are Nehru's views about poets and artists and their social predicament ?

3. What did Napoleon say upon his meeting with Goethe and why ?

4. What varied interests did Goethe have ?

5. On what evidence does Nehru consider Victor Hugo's career

remarkable ?

6. What did Balzac hope to achieve through his writings ?

7. What, according to Nehru, are the great obstructions on the path of one aspiring to be a poet or a writer ?

8. What had the Cambridge professor of English to say about the intellectual emancipation of the poor in England ? Why did he say that ?

9. What does Nehru have to say about the culture of his time and whom does he hold responsible for the prolonged cultural poverty in India ?

10. Why does Nehru quote Shelley's *The Mask of Anarchy* ?

11. Why would the grown-up Nehru not appreciate Scott's Waverley novels ?

COMPOSITION

1. Bring out Nehru's ideas on culture as stated in *Some Famous Writers*.

2. Why does Nehru think economic freedom is a pre-condition to the growth of culture in any society? Elucidate with examples from *Some Famous Writers*.

3. State Nehru's ideas about the philosophers and their writings as discussed in the chapter.

4. Write a note on the role of the youth in the Indian cultural scene today.

ON EDUCATION

GLOSSARY

dally : waste time; dawdle

commend : praise; recommend as worthy of notice

amateur : one who cultivates a particular study or art as a pastime, rather than as a profession

envisage : visualize

bigotry : obstinate or intolerant devotion to one's own religion or opinion

quaint : unusual or different in character; skilful, elegant

flaunt : displayed for show

refuge : shelter

marionette : a puppet moved by strings

TEXTUAL NOTES

Basic Scheme of Education : same as the Wardha Scheme of Education (See 'textual notes' to *The Cultivation of a Scientific Outlook*.)

COMPREHENSION

1. How literate are the majority of Indians according to Nehru?
2. How does Nehru find the expert's specialized way of looking at things full of shortcomings?
3. What does Nehru fear will happen if the educationists have no clear idea about the purpose of education?
4. How does Nehru define the ideals of education?
5. In what way does Nehru find the individual linked with his environment in his quest for advancement?
6. How does Nehru define the place of youth in the social structure?
7. With what end in view does Nehru advocate change in the social environment?
8. What kind of social change does Nehru believe will take place when the educational environment in the country changes?
9. How does Nehru visualize the role of a teacher in the ideal society of the future?
10. What kind of future does Nehru envisage for the Indian masses?
11. In what way does Nehru find the intellectuals cut off from reality?

COMPOSITION

1. Write on the aims and objectives of education, as stated by Nehru in *On Education*.
2. Why does Nehru find the world unpleasant? How does he propose to make it a more pleasant and just place for us to live in? Discuss.
3. Write a note on the present educational system in the country and suggest ways to inprove it.

STUDENTS AND POLITICS

GLOSSARY

authoritarian : dictatorial; favouring blind submission to authority
pompous : self-important; pretentious
hamstrung : disabled; crippled; powerless or useless
timidity : lacking in courage or self-confidence

COMPREHENSION

1. Which problems does Nehru describe as 'abstruse' and how well does he understand them?
2. Who, according to Nehru, can be called a keen citizen? Can he be a politician too?
3. What does Nehru want a student to do to save his formal education from going waste?
4. What, does Nehru say, is the purpose of the different *isms* in the

world? How does a person choose the right one for himself or herself?

5. How does a student benefit from his investigations into reality?
6. How does Nehru outline the student's goal? How should the student go about it?
7. What are Nehru's comments on the educational system in the India of his time?
8. Why and how does Nehru react to the 'spirit of authority' in universities?
9. What were the causes leading to a drought of adventurous men and women in the India of Nehru's time?
10. What is Nehru's advice to students who are passing through the formative years of their lives?

COMPOSITION

1. Write a note on the role of students in politics as Nehru sees it.
2. How does Nehru want students to prepare themselves to face life?
3. Briefly state your ideas about the role of the student community in nation building.

COTTAGE AND LARGE-SCALE INDUSTRIES

GLOSSARY

calamity : great misfortune; disaster
impetus : driving force, impulse, incentive
galvanize : to stimulate, excite or rouse as if by an electric shock
slavery : the state of being held in servitude as the property of another
indispensable : absolutely necessary; which cannot be done without

TEXTUAL NOTES

Ford Motor Company of the USA : one of the largest automobile manufacturers of the world

COMPREHENSION

1. Why does Nehru wish a few bombs would be dropped on Indian cities? Would you call him a war-monger?
2. Why is Nehru full of praise for the Chinese people?
3. What did the Chinese do to spread education in their country during the war years?
4. Why did the Chinese revive their cottage industries during the war years and what did they achieve by it?
5. What does Nehru consider to be the 'effect of the Japanese bombs' in China?
6. How does Nehru propose to achieve an equitable distribution of

wealth in India?

COMPOSITION

1. What does Nehru want the Indians to learn from the Chinese? How would such a lesson help Indians in solving their economic problems?
2. Why does Nehru think that cottage industries would be a boon to the Indian economy?

THE NEWSPAPERS AND THE COMMON MAN

GLOSSARY

weary : very tired
incessant : continual, uninterrupted
communion : interchange or act of sharing
wobble : to move unsteadily or uncertainly from side to side
crusading : any daring undertaking or concerted action to further a cause
zealously : ardently supporting something; enthusiastically
impede : obstruct, hinder
hobnob : associate, fraternize
squabble : a noisy, petty quarrel

TEXTUAL NOTES

the Bengal famine : of 1942-1943
Hindustani : language based on Hindi and Urdu and spoken in North India and Pakistan
Malaya : part of modern Malaysia
Reuters : British News Agency
Tass : Soviet News Agency

COMPREHENSION

1. What does Nehru say about his experience during his tour of the Indian countryside?
2. What suggestions does Nehru offer to the news agencies and reporters working in the city and why?
3. What does Nehru say about the conference?
4. Why does Nehru object to newspapers becoming industries?
5. What, according to Nehru, are the qualities a newspaper should consider essential for itself?
6. What does Nehru suggest the newspapers to do to avoid falling in peoples' estimation?
7. When and how does a newspaper get influenced by external elements?
8. Why does Nehru want the conference to insist upon the complete

freedom of news? What would be the benefits of such a policy?

9. What does Nehru think the government's policy should be vis-a-vis the newspapers?

10. What is the essence of Nehru's appeal to newspaper editors?

11. What personal difficulties did Nehru, as a politician, have with the press?

12. Why does Nehru advocate the transmission of news in Hindustani?

13. What does Nehru think of the English as well as the language newspapers in India?

14. Why does Nehru want a reduced difference in the pay-scales of the highest and lowest employees in any organization?

15. What does Nehru say are the shortcomings of the Indian-owned newspapers?

16. On what areas does Nehru want an Indian foreign news service to concentrate?

17. Why does Nehru suggest that newspapers develop greater contact with Asian nations?

COMPOSITION

1. Briefly describe Nehru's findings about the general state of affairs in the Indian press of his time and discuss his suggestions for its improvement.

2. What was the nature of Nehru's personal difficulties (as a politician) with the press? What were his ideas and suggestions to the conference for the successful working of the Indian press?

3. In what way does Nehru find the common man neglected by the Indian press? What guidelines does he offer for its improvement?

4. Write a note on the freedom of the press in present-day India.

THE NEW ASIA OF OUR DREAMS

GLOSSARY

isolationism : the policy of avoiding political entanglements with other countries

variegate : diversify, especially to mark with patches of different colours

antiquity : ancient times

efflorescence : the time of flowering; the period of developing and unfolding as if coming into flower

pan-Asia : all Asia; relating to all of Asia

forge : to form or bring into being, especially by an expenditure of some effort

pawn : small piece on a chessboard; a plaything; that which can be easily manipulated to further the purposes of another

enumerate : count the number of

tribulation : distress or suffering resulting from oppression or persecution

TEXTUAL NOTES

Sun Yat-sen : (1866-1925) Chinese revolutionary leader who did much to inspire and organize the movement that overthrew the Ch ing (Manchu) dynasty in 1911 to establish a republic. Through the Kuomintang party, he paved the way for the eventual reunification of the country.

Zaghlul Pasha : Saad Zaghlul Pasha (1859-1927) Egyptian political leader who founded the country's most important political party, the Wafd. This party was dissolved in 1956.

the Ataturk Kemal Pasha : Ghazi Mustapha Kemal Ataturk (1881-1938), Turkish nationalist and political leader who was instrumental in the fall of the Ottoman sultanate and, as President of the first Turkish Republic, founded modern Turkey.

COMPREHENSION

1. What does Nehru say was the result of the European domination of Asia?
2. What does Nehru see as the signs of change in the Asian scene at the end of the colonial era?
3. What part does Nehru say India would play in the new phase of Asian development?
4. Why does Nehru find Indian culture variegated?
5. How does Nehru say Indian culture crossed the frontiers of the country in the past? Where would one see the evidence of this today?
6. How does Nehru view the interaction of Irano-Arabic culture with the Indian culture as it then existed? What was the consequence of this interaction?
7. How does Nehru define and defend the purpose of the Conference he was addressing?
8. What does Nehru say will be the function of the Asian countries in the atomic age?
9. What, according to Nehru, should be the Asian contribution to the realization of the ideals of the UN?
10. In what way does Nehru find the Conference unique and significant?
11. Why does Nehru advise the Conference to avoid discussions on the internal politics of the member countries?
12. What measures does Nehru suggest for closer relations among the Asian countries and to what purpose?
13. What are the responsibilities, according to Nehru, of the Asian countries towards Africa?

14. What does Nehru feel about the conflicts and troubles in India as well as in other Asian countries?

COMPOSITION

1. Write a note on the changing situation in Asia, as viewed by Nehru, with special reference to the Indian scene.
2. Discuss Nehru's Pan-Asian concept and state how it would contribute to global peace in an atomic age.
3. Briefly analyze India's role in fostering the spirit of friendship in the Asian subcontinent.